Spring Awakening

Written in 1891, Wedekind's notorious play about adolescent
sexual repression had to wait three quarters of a century for a
public performance in Britain. The 1974 National Theatre
production was still only the second time the play had been seen
by any but a club audience, and a great deal of the strength of
this production derived from Edward Bond's much praised
translation, 'scrupulously faithful both to Wedekind's irony and
his poetry' (*The Times*). 'Edward Bond seems the right translator
for Wedekind', said *The Guardian*, 'in that his laconic style
exactly suits the original's innovatory one-sentence dialogue.'
Above all his text is actable, accurate and complete; and it has
been fully revised in the light of the production. This volume
includes a note on the play by Edward Bond, as well as a factual
introduction to Wedekind's life and work.

*The photo on the front cover, showing Peter Firth as Melchior
Gabor and Veronica Quilligan as Wendla Bergmann in the
National Theatre production, is by John Haynes.*

*The photo of Frank Wedekind on the back cover is reproduced
by courtesy of Bildarchiv Preussischer Kulturbesitz.*

Methuen's Theatre Classics

Buchner	DANTON'S DEATH (*English version by James Maxwell; introduced by Martin Esslin*) WOYZECK (*translated by John Mackendrick; introduced by Michael Patterson*)
Chekhov	THE CHERRY ORCHARD (*translated and introduced by Michael Frayn*) UNCLE VANYA (*translated by Pam Gems; introduced by Edward Braun*)
Euripides	THE BACCHAE (*English version by Wole Soyinka*)
Gogol	THE GOVERNMENT INSPECTOR (*translated by Kitty Hunter-Blair and Jeremy Brooks; introduced by Edward Braun*)
Gorky	ENEMIES THE LOWER DEPTHS (*translated by Kitty Hunter-Blair and Jeremy Brooks; introduced by Edward Braun*)
Granville Barker	THE MADRAS HOUSE (*introduced by Margery Morgan*)
Hauptmann	THE WEAVERS (*translated and introduced by Frank Marcus*)
Ibsen	BRAND A DOLL'S HOUSE AN ENEMY OF THE PEOPLE GHOSTS PEER GYNT (*translated and introduced by Michael Meyer*)
Jarry	THE UBU PLAYS (*translated by Cyril Connolly and Simon Watson-Taylor; edited by Simon Watson-Taylor*)
Molnar	THE GUARDSMAN (*translated and introduced by Frank Marcus*)
Synge	THE PLAYBOY OF THE WESTERN WORLD (*introduced by T.R. Henn*)
Tolstoy	THE FRUITS OF ENLIGHTENMENT (*translated and introduced by Michael Frayn*)
Wilde	THE IMPORTANCE OF BEING EARNEST (*introduced by Adeline Hartcup*) LADY WINDERMERE'S FAN (*introduced by Hesketh Pearson*)
Anon	LADY PRECIOUS STREAM (*adapted by S.I. Hsiung from a sequence of traditional Chinese plays*)

Frank Wedekind

SPRING AWAKENING

Translated by
EDWARD BOND
with introductions
by
EDWARD BOND
and
ELISABETH BOND

EYRE METHUEN
LONDON

This translation first published in 1980
by Eyre Methuen Ltd,
11 New Fetter Lane, London EC4P 4EE
Copyright in this translation and translator's introduction © 1980
by Edward Bond
Chronology and Introduction copyright © 1980
by Elisabeth Bond
Set in IBM Journal, by 𝓕\Tek-Art, Croydon, Surrey
Printed in Great Britain by
Fakenham Press, Fakenham, Norfolk
ISBN 0 413 47620 0

CAUTION

Frank Wedekind

1864 24 July: Emilie Wedekind, née Kammerer (1840 – 1915) gives birth in Hanover, Germany, to the second of her six children: Benjamin Franklin (Frank) Wedekind. Father: Friedrich Wilhelm Wedekind (1816 – 1888), doctor of medicine. The parents had just come back from America.

1872 Dr. Wedekind purchases Castle Lenzburg near Aarau in Switzerland where the family settles. Frank attends the 'Gemeindeknabenschule', then the 'Bezirksschule' from 1875, then from 1879 the 'Kantonsschule' in Aarau.

1879 He writes *Der Hänseken*, a children's epic for his youngest sister; writes poems and scenes (mostly parodies), in which he acts himself, for the school literary society.

1884 Matriculation. Enrols first at the University of Lausanne to study German philology and French literature. In the autumn, at his father's insistence, enrols at Munich to study law. Theatres, concerts, the circus remain his principal interests.

1886 Starts his first play. Meets Michael Georg Conrad and becomes a friend of Karl Henckell. Open quarrel with his father. November 1886 to July 1887: advertising manager of the Maggi soup firm near Zurich.

1887 Contact with the socialist group 'Young Germany' around Gerhart and Carl Hauptmann and John Henry Mackay. Starts to write for the *Neue Züricher Zeitung*. September: makes his peace with his father.

1888 11 October: sudden death of Dr. Wedekind.

1889 May – July: in Berlin. Then Munich. Contact with Otto Julius Bierbaum, Oskar Panizza, Hans Freiherr von Gumppenberg. Friendship with Willy Rudinoff and Richard Weinhöppel.

1890 To Easter 1891: writes *Spring Awakening*.

1891 December: to Paris, where he stays – with interruptions – until 1895.

1892 Fascinated by the theatre, ballet, variétés and the circus, whose way of life will help him to shape his philosophy. Friendship with Emma Herwegh; probably first contact with Willy Grétor. Begins 'Lulu' plays.

1894 January — June: in London. Meets Max Dauthendey, Georg Brandes; back in Paris, meets Albert Langen, his future Munich publisher.

1895 Returns to Germany: February in Berlin; summer in Munich. Tries to get his plays performed, without success. Autumn: Lenzburg, then Zurich; gives public readings mainly from Ibsen's plays, using the pseudonym Cornelius Minehaha. Starts his best known novel *Mine-Haha*. Langen publishes *Earth-Spirit*, the first of the 'Lulu' plays.

1896 Summer in Munich. Has more contributions than any other author in Langen's successful new periodical *Simplicissimus*.

1897 Contact with Kurt Martens of the Leipzig Literary Society. Readings.

1898 25 February: first performance in Leipzig of *Earth-Spirit (Erdgeist)*. Under the pseudonym 'Heinrich Kammerer', Wedekind plays the part of Dr. Schön. The director, Carl Heine, and his wife Beate along with Kurt Martens become lifelong friends. Heine tours *Earth-Spirit* with his 'Ibsen Theater': Wedekind is actor and theatre-secretary. Back in Munich Georg Stollberg, director of the Schauspielhaus, employs him as dramaturg, director and actor. On 29 October, after Munich premiere of *Earth-Spirit*, Wedekind is given a hint that he is going to be arrested because of some political poems published in *Simplicissimus* under the pseudonym 'Hieronymus Hobs'. Flees to Switzerland, then to Paris. Roughs out *The Marquis of Keith*.

1899 With *The Marquis of Keith* complete, he hands himself over to the German police in June. Accused of lèse-majesté and sentenced to seven months imprisonment, a sentence later commuted to confinement in a fortress ('Festungshaft'), in fact, Königstein near Leipzig. While Wedekind is still there, *The Singer*, also known as *The Tenor (Der Kammersänger)*, has its first night in Berlin (10 December).

1900 3 March: back to Munich. Contact with Max Halbe and his literary circle. 28 September: *The Love Potion (Der Liebestrank* or *Fritz Schwigerling)* premiered in Zurich.

1901 April: joins the new cabaret The Eleven Executioners ('Die Elf Scharfrichter') in Munich, and is the only member *not* using a pseudonym.

11 October: first night in Berlin of *The Marquis of Keith (Der Marquis von Keith)*.

1902 22 February: first night in Munich of *King Nicolo (So ist das Leben* or *König Nicolo)*.

1904 1 February: first night in Nuremberg of *Pandora's Box (Die Büchse der Pandora)* — the second, more hostilely received of the 'Lulu' plays. 23 March: confiscation of the first published edition.

1905 1 February: first night in Munich of *Hidalla* later entitled *Karl Hetman, the Dwarf-Giant (Karl Hetmann, der Zwergriese)*.

29 May: single club-performance in Vienna of *Pandora's Box*, organised by Karl Kraus, who plays Kungu Poti; Lulu: Tilly Newes; Jack the Ripper: Wedekind.

1906 1 May: Wedekind marries Mathilde (Tilly) Newes (1887-1970). Until 1908: residence in Berlin.

2 May: first night in Nuremberg of *Dance of Death (Totentanz)*, finally called *Death and Devil (Tod und Teufel)*, with the Wedekinds in the main roles.

20 November: Max Reinhardt's production of *Spring Awakening (Frühlings Erwachen)* opens at the Kammerspiele in Berlin. Wedekind is the Masked Man. It is to stay in the repertoire for twenty years and make Wedekind's name.

12 December: birth of first daughter, Anna Pamela.

1908 11 January: first night in Nuremberg of *Music (Musik)*.

2 April: first night in Munich of *The World of Youth (Die junge Welt)*. September: the Wedekinds finally settle in Munich.

1909 27 July: first night in Munich of *Censorship (Die Zensur)* as part of a Wedekind-cycle. Battles all the time with real censorship, which will go on until long after Wedekind's death.

Begins *Castle Wetterstein*.

1911 6 August: birth of second daughter, Fanny Kadidja.

20 December: first night in Munich of *Oaha*.

1912   June: first Wedekind-cycle in Berlin.
      30 November: first night in Munich of *Franziska*.

1914   24 January: first night in Berlin of *Simson*. Many
      honours on Wedekind's fiftieth birthday. A Wedekind-cycle
      in Berlin, another in Munich.
      29 December: appendicitis; operation not successful; wound
      doesn't heal. Hernia. More operations over the next few
      years. Wedekind continues to act and to write plays which
      get more and more abstract and are no longer performed
      today.

1915   25 March: death of Wedekind's mother.

1917   May to October: last tour with his wife as his partner in
      Switzerland.
      17 November: first night of *Castle Wetterstein* (*Schloß
      Wetterstein*), with Wedekind and Elisabeth Bergner.
      30 November: back to Munich. Given the news that his wife
      has tried to kill herself.

1918   2 March: last hernia operation.
      9 March: Wedekind dies in Munich. Tilly Wedekind lives on
      until 20 April 1970.

Introduction

'The flesh has its own spirit'
Frank Wedekind

His life was an adventure story. His legend was better known to his contemporaries than his work. His work was persecuted by the bourgeois and his best plays were not performed uncensored during his lifetime, in fact not until well after the Second World War. He didn't belong to any literary group or '-ism', but he opened a road which later generations have used.

He was the terror of the German bourgeoisie, a moralist who wore the mask of an immoralist. He was loved or hated, admired or despised, praised for being an apostle or condemned for being a devil. His enemies called him a lunatic, a criminal who wrote dirty, unsavoury plays. His admirers called him an idiot with a halo, God's fool. As an actor and director he was a phenomenon, as a man he was a magician. All his life he was faithful to his convictions and he never compromised. Even the fiercest battles with the censors couldn't stop him. The critic Alfred Polgar (1873-1955) called his plays 'battlefields over which the sun rises'.

When Frank Wedekind died in March 1918 at the age of 51, Bertolt Brecht, who was then 20, wrote his obituary in the *Augsburger Neueste Nachrichten*: 'Last Saturday night we sang his songs to the guitar as we swarmed down the Lech under the star-dusted sky . . . On Sunday morning we were horrified to read that Frank Wedekind had died the day before . . . Without actually seeing him buried I cannot conceive that he is dead. Like Tolstoy and Strindberg he was one of the great educators of modern Europe. His greatest work was his personality.'*

Brecht attended the funeral at the Munich Waldfriedhof. The different accounts of it read like a scene out of a Wedekind play.

*'Frank Wedekind' in *Brecht on Theatre*, ed. John Willett, London: Methuen, 1964, pp. 3-4.

The long train of mourners — family, friends, artists, intellectuals — wended its way through lines of Munich's bohemians and demi-monde. After the service in the burial hall the crowd broke up and galloped across the graves to get the best view. In the middle of it all a wild figure, waving and shouting directions, tried to film it. It was the poet Heinrich Lautensack, one of 'The Eleven Executioners', held back by a fellow 'Executioner', Erich Mühsam. After the long orations Lautensack forced his way to the grave, threw a wreath into it, broke down and cried: 'Frank Wedekind — your last pupil Lautensack!' Then he jumped into the grave. A few days later he was shut up in a mental asylum, where he died the following year.

Brecht held a private memorial celebration. He noted in his diary:

> They stood perplexed in tophats
> As if round the carcass of a vulture. Bewildered crows.
> And though they (sweating tears) tried hard
> They couldn't bury this juggler.

Wedekind remained one of Brecht's obsessions. It is recorded that he often quoted his words, partly by heart, imitating Wedekind's style as exemplary. He called his first son Frank after him. The expressionists also found inspiration in Wedekind, and he strongly influenced two other twentieth-century playwrights, Ödön von Horvàth and Friedrich Dürrenmatt. Dürrenmatt said: 'I don't think that a writer of our time can ignore Wedekind.' Wedekind in his turn felt himself to be indebted to Büchner and Heine. Alban Berg based his two great operas *Wozzek* and *Lulu* on plays by Büchner and Wedekind, respectively.

Wedekind was conceived in California and born in Germany on 24 July 1864. There he was registered as stateless under the name of Benjamin Franklin. He was the second of six children. His North-German father, a politically active, left-liberal doctor had emigrated to America after the failure of the 1848 revolution. In San Francisco a singer from South Germany visited his surgery as a patient. She was twenty-two and just divorced when they were married in 1862. He was forty-six. 'This fact appears to me to be not without significance', Wedekind wrote in one of his first autobiographical notes. He himself was almost forty-two when he

married. His wife was twenty. Both marriages were poisoned by
the husband's jealousy and clouded by their strange habits. The
pattern repeated itself in the third generation. Kadidja Wedekind
married the German expressionist playwright Carl Sternheim. He
was thirty-three years older than she, twice divorced and already
insane.

Wedekind's parents returned to Germany. Dr. Wedekind was
disgusted with Bismarck's anti-democratic politics and the
outcome of the Franco-German war of 1871/72. In 1872 he
purchased a castle called Lenzburg near Aargau in Switzerland.
Frank's childhood there was not unhappy although he felt
strongly the tension between his parents. This is made clear by a
letter written to his mother in defence of his younger brother
Donald, who later killed himself. He studied, not very
industriously, in the local schools and soon became a partly-liked,
partly-hated gangleader. In school reports he was called 'Franklin
Wedekind from San Francisco'. He was already writing and
performing scenes, poems and songs in the school's literary
society. When he sang he accompanied himself on the guitar. His
gift for friendship developed early. At home he was known as
'the thinker'. His letters are a marvellous key to his personality
and to the influences that helped to form him. In many of those
he wrote between the ages of seventeen and nineteen he deals with
the questions, problems and views that later took artistic shape in
Spring Awakening. He wrote on love, sexual desire, egotism,
society, the family, the education of children, literature,
religion, death — both seriously and humorously. All his life he
remained more interested in general social conditions than in the
politics to which his father was devoted.

When he returned from America his father had retired from
medical practice. In his library Frank must have found the new
ideas of the time in books by Marx, Engels, Bebel and Darwin. At
Lenzburg Dr. Wedekind became more and more of a
misanthropist. He shut himself up in the upstairs rooms, stamping
on the floor when he wanted something. The atmosphere must
have been nightmarish. In the winters it was so cold that the
water froze in the wash basins.

In those early years almost everything happened which later
bore fruit in Wedekind's life as a poet and a man. There was first

the intellectual influence of 'the philosophic aunt' Plümacher, a
pupil of the philosopher Eduard von Hartmann and a friend of
his mother. With her he held endless 'pessimistic discussions'.
Later she was replaced by 'the erotic aunt' Erika (Bertha Jahn),
the mother of a schoolfriend.

He matriculated in 1884 and went to Lausanne University for
a few months. He studied German philology and French
literature. Then he went to Munich and obeyed (without much
interest) his father's injunction to study law. Almost every
evening he went to the theatre, to concerts and — less
enthusiastically — to the opera. Opera was his mother's great
passion and later also his sister Erika's profession. He became
obsessed with the circus from the time of his first visit to it.

His decision to become a writer brought him into serious
conflict with his father, who made him responsible for his own
financial affairs. During a fierce row in the autumn of 1886 Frank
hit him. Frank was very upset at having done this but it took him
almost a year to apologise and make his peace. Anyhow by this
time he was sure about his future plans. He had written his
first play. He confessed to his worried mother: 'I now stand
on my own feet, and I have to be an egotist to make my own
place in the world. I'm convinced about my aim because I carry
my aim within me; that is to write something more than just
stories.' The letter was posted in Zurich where he'd met the most
influential poets and scientists of the 'Young Germany'
movement. One of his best friends, the lyric poet Karl Henckell,
had brought him into this circle of German exiles. Until 1890
their freedom in Germany was threatened by the 'socialist law'.
Their leading members were Carl and Gerhart Hauptmann. But
Wedekind soon fell out with these German 'Zola-ists' and their
theories. Gerhart Hauptmann was outraged by Wedekind's
sardonic songs to the guitar. He used Frank's private confessions
about his family life in his play *The Peace Celebration* (*Das
Friedensfest*), subtitled 'A Family Catastrophe'. Wedekind's
revenge was *Children and Fools,* later retitled *The World of Youth.*
In this play the hero, a fanatical poet, walks through the world
with a notebook and pencil. The message: When naturalism ends,
its representatives will be earning their bread as secret policemen.

By now Wedekind had proved himself as a writer of poems,

prose, sketches and plays. One of the plays was *The Waking of Elin* (*Elins Erweckung*), which dealt with some of the themes of *Spring Awakening*. He contributed articles to the *Neue Züricher Zeitung*, and in 1886 he became advertising manager of the Maggi soup firm. He also took on a job as secretary to a travelling circus.

After his father's sudden death in 1888 Wedekind gave up study. With his inheritance of 20,000 Swiss francs he felt free enough to travel and take up writing as his profession. He was addicted to city life and the following decade he travelled from city to city. First he went to Berlin. In 1889 it was the centre of German intellectual life; its literary culture was dominated by naturalists and realists. He had to leave as he couldn't provide the original documents to prove his nationality. But at least while he was there the fashionable literary circles had made him interested in the emerging question of the emancipation of women. He returned to Munich and started *Spring Awakening, A Children's Tragedy* in October 1890. It was finished by Easter 1891. In the autumn he published it at his own expense. It is the only play which he did not rewrite several times. During the time he wrote it, it is hardly mentioned in his letters and not at all in the first forty-three of his seventy-five notebooks, which are unpublished and now kept in the Munich State Library. Wedekind sent the script to a critic, stressing its moral standpoint. He was quite aware that there was no chance of getting it performed. But immediately after its publication *Spring Awakening* became well known to the younger generation.

Finally in 1906 Max Reinhardt, Germany's most famous producer between the early 1900s and 1933, put it on in the Kammerspiele of the Deutsches Theater in Berlin. However, crucial concessions had to be made to the censor: scenes four and six in Act Three had to be omitted, and Act Two scene three was mutilated to such an extent that Reinhart and Wedekind decided to cut it altogether. The caricatured names of the teachers had to be replaced by inoffensive ones. This was highly misleading as the idea of seeing them from the view-point of the pupils was obscured. And there were other problems: for example, young or child actors were unknown in the theatre of that time. An unexpected critic, the future commisssar Leon Trotsky made this point in 1908, stressing what an unaesthetic thing it is, 'when men

with shaved faces have to simulate children's breaking voices'.
Nevertheless this famous production was played 615 times over a
period of twenty years, with up to twenty changes in the cast.
Wedekind, having written the play when he was twenty-six, was
now seeing it staged for the first time at the age of forty-two. He
himself played the role of the Masked Man (forgetting his lines).
After this production he was at the peak of his success. Until the
First World War he was the most performed playwright in
Germany rivalled only by Gerhart Hauptmann.

But he had a long and difficult way to go before this
sensational breakthrough. Between 1892 and 1895 he lived
mainly in Paris, enjoying the boulevards, variétés, ballets and —
mostly — the circus. He built his philosophy of life on the image
of the circus and looked on himself as a tightrope-walker. In Paris
he met new and old friends of all sorts. One life-long friend was
Richard Weinhöppel, who later under the pseudonym Hannes
Ruch became the composer to the famous Munich cabaret 'The
Eleven Executioners'. The most fascinating friend was Willy
Rudinoff, actor, opera-singer, bird-song imitator, circus-mime,
black-face comic and painter. His pictures were exhibited in many
of the art centres of Europe. The Prince of Wales, later Edward
VII, was one of his admirers. Rudinoff had been to all continents.
He led the kind of life, based on following his instincts, which
Wedekind greatly admired but which *he* only created in fantasy,
being himself very conventional in his private life. Rudinoff had
shown Wedekind the underside of Munich. Now he took him to
the cabarets at Montmartre: there the dancers, singers and
cocottes fascinated him as much as the circus clowns and athletes.
Through a new friend, Emma, the widow of the revolutionary
poet Georg Herwegh, Wedekind got an entrée into the salons of
fashionable women writers.

All these experiences and many more are recorded in his autobiographical notes and in his sketches and pantomimes. They
finally crystallised in the 'Lulu' plays, started in 1892 as 'A
Monster Tragedy', then split into the two plays, *Earth-Spirit* and
Pandora's Box. Lulu is the incarnation of the 'innocent
immoralist' as Nietzsche saw it in his *Beyond Good and Evil*. Lulu
is 'the *real* animal, the *wild, beautiful* animal', as the Tamer points
out in the prologue. The role of the Tamer was sometimes played

by Wedekind. There is a gripping photograph of him in the part,
but unfortunately we haven't got his voice on a record. 'Lulu' was
Wedekind's second masterpiece and it caused him his toughest
battles. It was rejected and banned many times before it was finally
printed and staged. But during Wedekind's lifetime it was not
often seen except in club performances.

Nevertheless *Earth-Spirit* was the first of Wedekind's plays to
be performed. This was in 1898 at a Leipzig Literary Society
meeting. It was directed by Carl Heine and Wedekind, who used
his grandfather's name, Heinrich Kammerer, as a pseudonym.
Wedekind also acted the role of Dr. Schön. Carl Heine and his
wife Beate with whom Wedekind exchanged affectionate letters
soon became his most devoted friends and fought on his behalf
when he was attacked.

In 1894, having run out of money, he spent the first half of
the year in London, apparently as the secretary of the Danish
painter, art-dealer and congenial forger Willy Grétor. Grétor, the
most eccentric of his friends, often helped him to survive the
financial crises that followed when his inheritance began to run
out. Wedekind found London provincial, tasteless and boring,
without sun and glamour, and its women unattractive and sexless.
His life normally started at night, and what annoyed him most
was that 'at twelve in the evening one is sentenced to bed by the
police'.

A few years later he really was sentenced. Grétor had
introduced him to Albert Langen, a courageous but dubious
character, who had founded a publishing firm in Munich. (The
firm was later joined by Georg Müller and Langen-Müller is still
one of the leading German publishers.) During the frustrating
times when nobody dared to perform his anti-naturalistic plays,
Wedekind earned a living by reciting — especially Ibsen, whom he
did *not* regard as a naturalistic playwright. Again he used a
pseudonym, 'Cornelius Minehaha'. Langen risked publishing
Earth-Spirit in 1895. Then he founded his extraordinarily
successful periodical *Simplicissimus*. It contained a kind of
sophisticated, liberal mixture of satire, politics and eroticism.
Many leading European writers wrote for it, among them Knut
Hamsun, the brothers Mann, Rilke, Schnitzler and Hofmannsthal.
The illustrators included Gulbransson, Thöny, Thomas Theodor

Heine. During its first year Wedekind's work appeared in its pages more often than that of any other author.

In 1898 his life seemed to have changed for the better. He was now engaged as dramaturg, director and actor at the Munich Schauspielhaus, and *Earth-Spirit* had its second production. During the performance Wedekind was given a hint that he was going to be arrested. He had published some political poems in *Simplicissimus*. The most offensive of these concerned Kaiser Wilhelm's colonial expansionist trip to Palestine. Wedekind was writing under the pseudonym Hieronymus Jobs. Langen had encouraged him and assured him that there was no danger. But the police found the handwritten originals in the editor's office. Wedekind fled to Zurich and later to Paris. Langen had already fled before him.

In exile Wedekind roughed out the play he always thought of as his best, *The Marquis of Keith*, a masterly constructed, cynical satire about a swindler (whose character was based on Grétor). The last sentence gives its essence: 'Life is a switchback'. As soon as he'd finished it he handed himself over to the German police.

After six weeks imprisonment the court sentenced him to a further seven months imprisonment and then commuted this to confinement in a fortress, a more honourable punishment than imprisonment. In Königstein, a beautiful castle on a hill near Leipzig, he wrote his best known novel *Mine-Haha, or The Education of Young Girls* 'in considerable comfort'. While he was still locked up his most popular and most often performed one-act play, *The Singer,* had its first night in Berlin. He'd written it in 1897 when he was staying in Dresden with his sister Erika. She was then a well-known concert and opera singer. She helped him out of one of his many financial crises. Her patronising attitude to him is satirised in *The Singer*, but her identity is camouflaged behind that of a male singer. In his later career as an actor the part of 'The Singer' became one of Wedekind's most popular roles. Others were the Marquis of Keith, Hetmann in *Hidalla* and Dr. Schön in the 'Lulu' plays. In 1913 he provided a five-act version of *Lulu* which was to be played in one evening. Almost fifty years later his daughter Kadidja made another version and started a Wedekind renaissance with it. It was then that the critics, who had at the most been expecting a history lesson, discovered a 'new' playwright.

After his release from Königstein in March 1900 Wedekind clutched at another straw, one which he'd actually helped to grow. During his time in Paris he had become very interested in the new kind of literary cabaret. He had passed this interest on to his friends in Berlin and Munich as early as 1895. At the turn of the century Otto Julius Bierbaum's slogan 'Life saturated with art' was being put into practice. The first German cabarets were rather naive imitations of their Montmartre originals. But soon after 'The Eleven Executioners' opened in Munich, Wedekind became their main attraction and the first important German cabaret artist. By now he was the only member *not* using a pseudonym. His songs protested against bureaucracy, religion and the prostitution of bourgeois marriage. His song 'Ilse' which directly refers to a girl in *Spring Awakening*, and also to the Lulu image, made the only *chansonneuse* in the group, Marya Delvard, famous overnight. Heinrich Mann recollects Wedekind's appearance on stage as puzzling and weird: 'The ribboned lute in clumsy hands, he faced the aesthetic world of his time . . . Small steps, "I come, you shan't escape me". A strongly etched head with the profile of a Caesar, the head bowed in mischief, ragged short hair. Offensive, twitching eyes . . . Irritability and sudden sadness. Strumming as if perturbed, then the performance. Nasal, sharp, shrilling — but in pauses full of meaning, the singer twisted and hunched behind his mental barrier.' Mann's description also gives us a picture of Wedekind as an actor. Even his enemies and fiercest critics had to admit his diabolical, magical presence. In her memoirs the actress Tilla Durieux, who had played opposite him, called him 'a lofty clown', 'a moralistic cynic', 'a devilish poor devil'. She says that Wedekind 'the dilettante, the ridiculed, was the strongest of us . . . Out of his heavy body his voice sounded with an abruptness and fire which only prophets have'. There are similar accounts from many others who knew or saw him.

After 1900 he toured with the cabaret, wrote three more plays, another novel, many songs and several fragments. In December 1902 *Earth-Spirit* was produced at Reinhardt's Kleines Theater in Berlin. It became a success with the intellectuals but Wedekind was still not widely recognised as a major playwright. After the

first night of this production the well-known actor Friedrich
Kayssler wrote on a postcard to Wedekind 'You have throttled
the naturalistic monster of probability and brought the element
of play back to the theatre.'

This was true, and Wedekind became more and more convinced
that in an age of touring star actors he had to train them to play
in his anti-naturalistic style. So when he was almost forty years
old he took acting and dancing lessons and a postal course in
make-up.

In 1905 his time finally came. A Wedekind-cycle with the
author in the leading roles was performed in Nuremberg.
Germany's most influential theatre critic, Alfred Kerr, had already
praised him. In Vienna the poet and satirist Karl Kraus — Kerr's
antagonist — arranged the first production of *Pandora's Box* in a
club performance. He rented a theatre for one night. The rising
actress, Tilly Newes, who was then nineteen, was Lulu. Wedekind
was Jack the Ripper. She immediately became his idol and ideal
partner. That autumn he got her a contract to play with him in
Berlin. He wrote to his mother on 7 May 1906: ' I've just gone
through the most strenouos time of my life. In eight days two
first nights and a wedding.' He'd married Tilly on the first of May
and on the second both of them played in the first performance in
Nuremberg of his *Dance of Death* (later renamed *Death and Devil*
to distinguish it from Strindberg's play). The play was a success.
But in Vienna Karl Kraus wasn't allowed to stage it even in a club
performance. Battles with censorship went on in Germany and
many other places in the following years. The Wedekinds settled
in Berlin and were in demand by the theatres of all the main cities.
As a director Frank converted some of the best actors to his anti-
naturalistic style. At the end of 1906 Tilly gave birth to their first
daughter Pamela. In 1911 there was a second daughter, Kadidja.

Wedekind enjoyed his fame. He wanted his wife to appear only
in his plays. The marriage was not an easy one. In her honest and
full autobiography, *Lulu: the Role of my Life*, Tilly tells of their
difficulties, his unjust jealousy, his fear of being too old for her,
the way of life which he had developed as a bachelor, his working
habits. He still wrote plays, year after year. Most of them were
written at night in pubs and coffee houses. Then he slept in his
room till lunchtime. Tilly was loyal to him, appreciating his

kindness. She even offered to take in his two illegitimate sons, one of them by Frida, Strindberg's second wife, and the other by Hildegarde Zellner. Wedekind had had a brief contact with Strindberg in 1894. They had not got on very well, obviously because of their mutual obsession with but different outlook on women. Tilly says that almost all of Wedekind's vitality went into his work. This is proved by the remarks of several of his contemporaries who pointed out that his passion came from his brain. He lived his motto 'the flesh has its own spirit' in his own way. In his work women are either 'noble beautiful animals' or they are perverted like the Countess Geschwitz in the 'Lulu' plays. In contrast his men embody the passion of spirit, even when they are ruthless seducers. Constantly changing constellations of these images create Wedekind's grotesque, comic-horror effects.

In 1908 the family finally settled in Munich. Wedekind loved it. He decorated the flat himself, especially his own huge study. According to Tilly everything from the carpets and curtains to the furniture (which Wedekind painted himself) was red with a few patches of yellow. He was an ideal father. Much to the amusement of his daughters he invented his own coat of arms, three women's legs in different colours. Over his writing desk he hung the famous painting of Tilly as Lulu. (It was destroyed by bombs in the last war.) Around the walls were all the instruments he'd taught himself to play: lute, mandoline, guitar, and various percussion instruments. There were many books, pieces of office equipment, props from his plays such as a drum and a huge ball. Tilly said that the whole room looked 'like a circus arena'.

On his fiftieth birthday Wedekind received many honours. One of them was a book with contributions by leading artists and intellectuals. And there were two Wedekind-cycles, one in Berlin and one in Munich.

In autumn he fell ill with appendicitis. The operation wasn't successful. The scar wouldn't heal. Until his death almost three and a half years later he was repeatedly operated on. There is some suggestion that it might have been cancer. But he continued to perform and write. His late plays became more and more abstract, variations on his old themes. During these years of agony he controlled himself in a very disciplined way. Elisabeth Bergner,

who in November 1917 acted opposite him in the first
performance of *Castle Wetterstein*, wasn't aware of how ill he was.
A last operation took place on 2 March 1918. On 9 March he was
dead. Wedekind's deathmask shows a beautiful face with a slightly
mocking smile. Eight years before, Thomas Mann had stated:
'History will one day say that, in an era compounded of senility,
puerility and feminity, Wedekind was the only *man*'.

When Wedekind wrote *Spring Awakening* it was the first time
in his life he felt free. He remembered that he started to write the
first three scenes without any overall plan. Then suddenly this
strange play took shape. It broke through all the clichés of the
theatre of his time, both in what he said and in how he said it. In
every scene there is an element of autobiography. But there is at
the same time a panorama of the growth of adolescence. The
individual problems of puberty, of adapting to the adult world, of
the sacrifice of the needs of childhood, of frustration and of
moments of happiness in both sexes. Melchior and Moritz are the
two sides of Wedekind's personality, shown trapped in the social
cage he describes so brilliantly. Two of his school-friends had
killed themselves, and even the words 'That boy wasn't mine'
were spoken by the father of one of them.

Wedekind played the Masked Man in the first production.
Nine rehearsals had already taken place before he was allowed to
attend: 'I found there a really horrible tragedy in the grandest
dramatic style. I tried to do the most I could to bring out the
sense of humour, especially in the scenes with Wendla, and in all
the scenes with her mother, as well as in the last scene; I tried to
develop the intellectual, the playful elements and to dampen
down the passionate elements, including those in the last scene
at the churchyard. I believe that the play is more gripping the
more harmless, sunny, laughing the performance.' Wedekind
came back to this essential point when he was writing to his
teacher, the actor Fritz Basil, who took over the part of the
Masked Man in Munich: 'Until Reinhardt's production the play
was looked on as pure pornography. Now they've plucked up
courage to see it as the driest school pedantry. But still no one's
able to see humour in it.'

If people had looked closely they would have discovered that
Wedekind was neither a teacher nor a preacher but a genuine

educator. He had educated himself to a moral understanding and had learned the clarity which makes his plays models of their type. In *Spring Awakening* he contrasts the world of puberty with the world of bourgeois morality. Throughout his life he studied and analysed social behaviour. What his average contemporaries found so difficult to understand was the fact that he did not wallow in naturalistic details or symbolist fog. He had found a style which was as far from the usual theatre pathos as it was from the underacting which was just then becoming fashionable. As a playwright, actor and director he increasingly followed his own interpretation. In the preface to *The Singer* he asks 'the professional actor' for 'tempo, passion and intelligence'. He rejected fashionable over-designing, elaborate costumes and too many (or too few) props. Nothing should distract the audience from the words. These should have absolute priority. His wife Tilly, not always happy about his adamant views on acting, said that he actually longed for 'the trained-animal act'.

Structurally *Spring Awakening* was well ahead of its time. But it also marked a return to the techniques of Germany's best classical playwrights. There are short, tense scenes such as those found in Lenz, Grabbe, Büchner — and monologues which recall Goethe and Schiller. Following Heine he used the method of first creating and then destroying a lyrical, sentimental, poetic mood. In *Spring Awakening* he made striking use, for his time, of the mosaic-like alternation of indoor and outdoor scenes. Light and darkness, bright and dim; scenes between adolescents and adults, boys and girls, boys and boys, girls and girls, mother and daughter, wife and husband, teacher and pupil. Even the smallest parts such as Wendla's sister or the locksmith are sharply etched and ineradicable. Although the sequence of events is not tightly woven, the impact gives the clear pattern of the life of a small town about 1890. The churchyard scene was truly original. On the one hand Melchior is invited by Moritz to die, as Don Giovanni was invited by the Commendatore, and on the other hand he is lured back to life by the Masked Man, as Faust was by Mephistopheles. Wedekind wanted to give life, with all its mysteries and uncertainties, priority over death.

Fritz Kortner (1892 - 1970), an actor and, with Piscator and Jessner, one of the most influential directors of his time, was known and feared for his cynical and often ruthless remarks. But he remembers in his memoirs that he fainted and had to be carried out of a performance of *Spring Awakening* when he was fifteen.

Wedekind's mother loathed the play. She was the model for Frau Gabor, Melchior's seemingly sensible, understanding mother, who in the end is also his persecutor.

The writer and director Berthold Viertel (1885 - 1953), who during his war-time exile in America performed Brecht in English and German, has a chapter on Wedekind in his *Writings on Theatre*. There he says: 'When we were young Frank Wedekind was the Masked Man of his (our) *Spring Awakening*. With a satanic sneer as polite as an abyss and full of cold melancholy he introduced us to the mysteries of reality which began where the views of the pacifying poets end. This was the turn of the century. Bourgeois ideas lay in their agony.'

ELISABETH BOND-PABLÉ
1980

Select Bibliography of Books in English

Translations of Wedekind's plays:

Tragedies of Sex, translated and introduced by S.A. Eliot, Jnr, London: Henderson, n.d.; New York: Boni & Liveright, 1923. Includes *Spring Awakening, Earth-Spirit, Pandora's Box, Damnation!*

Five Tragedies of Sex, trans. F. Fawcett & S. Spender, intro. L. Feuchtwanger, New York: Theatre Arts, n.d.; London: Vision, 1952. Includes *Spring Awakening Earth-Spirit, Pandora's Box, Death and Devil, Castle Wetterstein.*

The Lulu Plays and other Sex Tragedies, trans. Stephen Spender, London: Calder, 1972. Includes *Earth-Spirit, Pandora's Box, Death and Devil, Castle Wetterstein.*

King Nicolo in *The Genius of the German Theatre,* ed. Martin Esslin, London & New York: Mentor, 1968.

Lulu, translated and abridged by Peter Barnes, London: Heinemann Educational, 1971.

The Singer in *Frontiers of Farce,* trans. Peter Barnes, London: Heinemann Educational, 1977.

The Marquis of Keith in *From the Modern Repertoire, Series Two,* ed. Eric Bentley, Bloomington: Indiana University Press, 1952.

Books about Wedekind and his era:

Best, Alan, *Frank Wedekind,* London: Oswald Wolff, 1975.

Garten, H.F., *Modern German Drama,* London: Methuen, 2nd ed., 1964, pp. 87-96.

Gittleman, Sol, *Frank Wedekind,* No. 55 in Twayne's World Authors series, New York: Twayne, 1969.

Pascal, Roy, *From Naturalism to Expressionism, German Literature and Society 1880-1918*, London: Weidenfeld & Nicolson, 1974.

Spalter, Max, *Brecht's Tradition*, Baltimore: Johns Hopkins, 1967.

Willett, John, *Expressionism*, London: Weidenfeld & Nicolson, 1970.

A Note on the Play

Spring Awakening is partly about the misuse of authority. All the adult men in the play work in the professions (except the locksmith and Fastcrawler). They are members of institutions that are part of the state, and they base their work on the state's ethos and teach its doctrines. The judge is a verbal sadist, the doctor a quack, the head of the reformatory an upholder of the nineteenth-century philosophy of brutality-and-christianity, and the teachers fact-machines that scheme but can't think. Their inefficiency as human beings and their inefficiency as functionaries involve each other — which is why authoritarian states are wasteful and finally collapse.

Our society is highly inefficient; the modern, scientific, industrial state is probably the most inefficient culture that's ever existed. Anyone who's worked in a modern office knows that office workers spend as much of their time as they can avoiding work and daydreaming. And when factory workers go through their minute mechanical operations they sustain themselves not through an act of will or pleasure but only because the conveyor belt or hopper pushes them into activity. That's an obviously inefficient use of human beings, and it leads to even greater inefficiency — to a breakdown in personal and social lives. There is no human reward in such work, only wages. That is not an acceptable recompense for a life of industrial captivity. A modern factory puts its workers in chains. It's designed to use machinery with the utmost possible efficiency — in the narrowest mechanical sense — but it uses human beings with almost total inefficiency. People are not mentally, physically or emotionally designed to be machine watchers, least of all when the machines belong to others. And although people can adapt to many things, when the adaptations needed are extreme and unrewarding they lead to irrationalism, nervousness and sickness. So factories are constantly shut down by strikes and hampered by works-to-rule and demarcation disputes. There isn't even any good reason to *try* to co-operate when not only the luxuries but even the basic securities go to the exploiters. The same irrationalism and sickness occur throughout society and create crime and violence. These are warning signs. When people are so organised that their culture becomes irrational and trivial, their entertainment facile and sentimental, their politics xenophobic and racialist, and their morality a sycophantic respect for the law and order of self-perpetuating elites, then they are not *human* beings. A tiger doesn't have to choose to be a tiger, but a human being has to choose to be human or else he is only an over-efficient animal. And that means he is an inefficient man, and dangerous to himself and others. Our society makes it difficult to choose to be human because we don't have a culture (in the sense I shall describe later) but only an organisation.

The adults in *Spring Awakening* are dangerous. Obviously they destroy or brutalise their children. But what of themselves and their pleasures? A miserable sort of sex between unhappy women and unfulfilled men; gloomy drinking at funerals; pride, arrogance and isolation. The judge says 'I see the future so grey, so overcast', and the priest calls life a cross. They are dangerous not only to themselves but to everyone. They exist only through conflict and their conflict doesn't come from an analytical passion but is a wish for destruction. The teachers fight about trivialities; they are afraid to question anything more important. Their satisfaction is associated with their own or others' pain. Their conflict can't end because they're each at war with themselves. They must either destroy themselves or create new enemies. They are typical authoritarian men: sly, gringing, mindless zombies to those over them, and narrow, vindictive, unimaginative tyrants to those under them. And, as they never see those under them with imagination, they don't even really 'exist' for them! If their masters say that those under them should be exploited more, or exterminated, the zombies carry out the orders. They concentrate all their imagination on those over them, and live in a rich and intricate mental world in which they either glamorise their overlords or secretly accuse them of extravagant, endless malice and deviousness. This is the character of the servants of fascism. Evil is made metaphysical so that it need not be fought. Praise and blame become the same thing, because fear has paralysed action.

The simple, brutal facts of exploitation and coercion are ignored.
    These men make wars possible. They are the means if not the
cause. The murder and suicide of children in *Spring Awakening*
shock us. But what of those who survive? If we place the play at
the turn of the century, they were killed off in the First World
War — and that was called heroism. Can a society survive having
military heroes? When Kennedy got out of the Cuba confrontation
without using nuclear weapons, some of the American military
were sorry. That's only an extreme example of the present crisis
in the relationship between force and politics. In the past a state's
security depended on its ability to control its enemy's army, now
it depends on its ability to control its own. And what of the
civilian hero? In a technological society everything depends on
conformity to routine, in work and leisure. Glamorisation of the
stiff-upper-lipped, religious, patriotic, law-abiding TV hero — the
paragon of watch committees and pro-censorship campaigners —
is an incitement to thuggery, violence and civil disorder. How
else can the culturally deprived imitate the initiative of the public
hero, how else dissolve their intellectual bewilderment in action so
as to create the illusion of a heroic solution? — except by kicking
someone as innocent as themselves. In a non-culture it's not
pornography that corrupts and produces violence — at the worst it
only leads to hedonistic quietism — but the glamorisation of
public-school, clean-cut moral virtue. An undemocratic
technology creates this paradox: the closest most members of that
society can get to recreating in themselves the pose and dynamic
of a glamorised police force is by breaking the law. Paradoxes
such as this are at the heart of our cultural decay.

Many of the young people in *Spring Awakening* are already like
their elders. They have the same brash egoism, almost the same
brutality — not quite, because it is still nakedly sneering and not
yet covered with fake morality. All these boys will go to the
trenches and die with the same obedience they learned at school
and were rewarded for with exam passes. Education in that sort of
society is a preparation not for life but quite literally for death.
And so is ours — if it doesn't leave us sane and free enough to ask
why human animals who have been trained to obey like
laboratory rats are sitting in front of buttons that can begin

nuclear destruction.

This sort of discipline is synonymous with mindlessness. We hide this by talking of 'self-discipline' and of freedom being 'the knowledge of necessity', but in a society that is more destructive than creative that is certainly not true. Self-discipline, in this society, means coercing yourself instead of paying an official to coerce you. It isn't self-responsibility. Self-responsibility always stresses moral understanding, it defines even its certainties by questions. No *human* being can abdicate this responsibility for the sake of discipline. That doesn't mean they cannot co-operate. In fact only in this way can co-operation be efficient. The discipline imposed by authority, no matter how subtly, is inefficient. It wastes energy and stops initiative.

Disciplined people always judge by appearances, and they are educated not only to do what they are told but to believe they *want* to do it. Some children try to escape this discipline. Often the most alert and intelligent children are regarded by their teachers as the least able. Moritz isn't a fool. He sees under the surface — itself a socially undesirable thing to do. But he isn't robust. He withdraws into fantasies and dreams. These are called poetry, and it would be inhuman to deny them to a prisoner. The danger is that instead of using them as private comfort for his anguish, he fantasises reality. In Act one, scene four, it's *not* true that he's passed the exam — yet. But it *is* true that he could have run away — at least as much as Röbel or any other student. In a similar way authority corrupts art and turns it away from reality. The ineffectual pessimism which Moritz describes in the last scene — sonorous, world weary, smiling serenely over the tragedies and absurdities of the world — has great academic respectability. It's the cliché that poets write for tomorrow — about as possible as shaving in a mirror not yet made. It's Auden saying all the left-wing poetry of the thirties didn't save one Jew from the gas chambers. It can immediately be seen to be a false attitude.

Melchior is even worse than Moritz: he's normal. Only the abnormal fit into polite society. He is a threat to it. He is also another instance of the ultimate justice in human affairs: his father the judge, the defender of law and order or social injustice, has a criminal son — that is, a normal son who wishes to live in the knowledge of what he is and accept responsibility for it. But even he has been smeared over with Nietzschean melodrama. He has a philosophy of egoism that denies moral discrimination. But it is only an adolescent pose, made plausible to him because he sees the hypocrisy of public morality. In the last scene of Act one, when he asks Wendla about charity, he doesn't attack moral differences. The poor and unemployed would be right to hate Wendla's parents. That would be rational. (I leave out the question of forgiveness because that's useless in a slum.) He is only objecting to the moral judgements of the Public God, who condemns people for doing what they can't help doing. And there is a twist: Wendla *would* like to visit the poor because it made her *un*happy. Discipline is joy through misery. The paradox is another of those our society lives by. The irony of the scene is that authoritarians must hold (as Wordsworth did) that god·created the poor for the moral education of mankind, just as he created lepers that saints might have sores to kiss.

The play isn't out of date. It becomes more relevant as our armies get stronger, our schools, prisons and bombs bigger, our means of imposing discipline themselves more disciplined and more veiled, and our self-knowledge not much greater. The aim of the education shown in this play is to stop people asking questions. That's also a foundation of the consumer society. Consume, and don't ask what or where or why or anything at all except for more. There may seem to be a great difference between Wedekind's society and ours. There *is* a difference in technique. It's more efficient to replace naked force with consumer rewards. But even these are backed by force. The comfort is only apparent, the future remains insecure. People are encouraged, but when this fails, they are still forced. Modern technological industry offers very little security. The state and commerce have become one inter-related machine that must be kept running at all costs. People can't fall back on the natural environment when their society is unacceptable to them, as drop-outs in feudal or primitive societies could do, at least for a time. The total-machine *is* the environment. The self-autonomy of drop-outs in our society is really only the self-autonomy of parasites, and our society is clearly so arranged that its parasites live off the poor not the rich.

The only purpose of our society is to keep the total-machine running. Human objectives are sacrificed to this mechanical imperative. There are examples of this everywhere. Why does a working-class father work in a factory to make bombs to drop on other working men's children? He doesn't even have the incentive of increasing his dividend. So has he no moral sense? That judgement is easy. What else can he do? He must take what work there is or his family will live in poverty — perhaps not in hunger and cold, but in a deeper poverty, the cultural poverty that causes crime, child battering, family violence, drunkenness, poor education, intellectual stagnation, wasted time, and social persecution and rejection. He is forced to act immorally — and rewarded for doing so — because he has no democratic responsibility for his own life. He can't ask questions because he's never allowed to choose answers. Those are left to the people who run the total-machine, and they won't provide moral answers because they are only concerned with keeping the total-machine running. So ironically the working people who are denied democratic responsibility are often the ones who insist on the total-machine being kept running at all costs — it's the only security they have. Right-wing politicians take this as proof that the working class isn't interested in moral questions. They don't see that pseudo-democracy is the political organisation that makes moral initiative impossible — at least as an integral part of the working of the state. And that really it is only another aspect of that extraordinary and optimistic truth: human emotions and mind, rationality and physical functioning are so inter-related that only morally active people can sustain a society that is efficient, whose activity isn't just the frenzy of an explosion. Without freedom any organisation becomes sterile because there is no moral choice, no emotional commitment and no physical stability. The one leads to the other.

We live in a scientific age. We ought to educate our children well. Most children are taught lies. They are told that life has meaning and purpose, that their own actions count and so they must be careful what they do, that they must treat life as an adventure, and that they live in a democracy. But the children who go to the barrack-schools in our cities know that they will pass dull lives (the excretory metaphor is intended) in grey, ugly cities, will only be able to show initiative when they strike, and will have no democratic responsibility for the future and welfare of even their own family. So they can't learn the culture they're offered. You might as well offer them the mores of ancient Rome. Our behaviour is as absurd as if we tried to teach Latin to children who will spend their lives in industrial slums. We *do* still teach them a dead culture, a dead religion and dead social myths.

What is culture? Human beings must have a culture, it's a biological necessity. We have mechanical, mental and emotional abilities. We see, hear, remember, we have manipulating hands and a subtle posture, we can trust, love and so on. All this creates a wide experience that pours into a child and must be organised so that it can cope with the world — that is, have a technology — and live in harmony with others; and the two together make a culture. A culture is what you live by, and it makes human living possible. But if it's going to be lived by it must be tested against reality. (This is a peculiarity of children which adults can lose by going privately mad, or by going politically mad and adopting fantasy political cultures such as fascism. This, like all attempts to live outside reality, ends in disaster.) The culture offered to children in our city barrack-schools — when they are too cowed to play truant — doesn't stand this test. So it would be irrational of children to accept it. And as the human young must have a culture, must have attitudes and beliefs, founded on experience, that enable them to form a community with the people they live with — so they are left to their own devices and develop a culture of their own. What happens in our great technological cities in this flowering of the age of science? Our children learn the culture of the outlaw. It is the only culture open to them. It is often a brutal culture, and of course this leads to calls from the law-abiding for more violence to deal with it. In this way society is doubly brutalised by its neglect. The culture of the outlaw flourishes in our cities, and — if technology hadn't made our situation dangerous and true democracy essential — that would even be a good sign, because it would show that the young are better judges of reality than the old and still reject the spurious.

Technology is a giant that must be made to work to the human scale. Factories haven't yet been designed to do this. They don't

even develop the loyalty of mining communities, because there is
no human pride in the work they offer, no physical or mental
skill, only a few mechanical tricks. When people live and work in
ways that, in spite of all the human capacity to adapt, are still
unsuitable for them, when their work and entertainment make no
demands on their creativity, so that their creative abilities aren't
used and challenged, then they work badly and can't co-operate
in a community. Why did men die so obediently in the First World
War? One reason is that they were already living lingering deaths.

There will soon be a worsening of the technological crisis and
more political unrest. The total-machine will stall for many
reasons. Human beings aren't bits of mechanical machinery and
therefore they don't fit easily into the total-machine. This
activates their defensive aggression. And commercial technology
not only destroys its material resources, it also stimulates rampant
consumer greed and so destroys its social basis. It can only offer
more and more rewards, and in a crisis its promises aren't kept
and so there is still more fear and aggression. And anyway even if
prosperity continued, the total-machine could still only be
maintained by offering more rewards — which become more
and more unrewarding, even a nuisance! Prosperity is as corroding
as crisis, success as destructive as failure — another of the
paradoxes that threaten us. Our system uses human beings so
inefficiently that it must destroy itself either through success or
failure. The usual answer to all this is force. Strikes are made
illegal, the punishment of hooliganism is made harsher. But the
inflationary leap-frogging of law-and-order and unrest-and-violence
can't restore balance. It is itself a part of the crisis we're in. We're
trapped in a cultural inflation of threat and counter-threat, and
this conflict can't create its own solution. The solution, either
good or bad, must be imposed from outside. And if it's good, it
can't be sanctioned by our present social morality. Either way
our present social system must be replaced.

Politicians will probably try to stabilise society by using
technology directly against their citizens (as rewards are either no
longer available or don't work). They will have the deepening
crisis as a justification, and conventional morality will be on their
side. Instead of creating a society in which people can live happily,
which has till now been the justification for the force used in

politics, they will try to create people who will fit into their society — people who are small total-machines. It's usually thought this would be done by genetics, selection, open indoctrination. Perhaps these ideas are too crude. They would require legislation that would publicly demonstrate what was going on. Our democracy could be gutted in simpler ways, even without the spoken or conscious intention of doing it. The control of ideas, information, working and living environments, entertainment, the limitation of the right to organise, and heavier penal sanctions — these are probably the only things that would be necessary. The members of the total-machine need not be tranquillised or peaceful; obedience and consent can be obtained through anger and fear. Either way, technology and science would be used to produce sycophantic loyalty, aggressive jingoism and belligerent social conformity. That is of course an irrational use of science. But science is rational only in its methods, not in its social application. The use of scientific truth has to be watched as closely as the disposal of sewage. The first responsibility lies with those who create it. We know that if society is going to work we mustn't defecate on the streets; yet scientists still defecate knowledge on the White House carpet and protest when they're called irrational. When there are no sane political controls on the use of science, what is the justification for society's decision to put scientific truth in a category higher than moral truth?

I think, anyway, that a political equilibrium created by technology would fail. I don't believe in human robots or technological ants. The only viable solution is to recreate the possibility of genuine human choice, to have a real instead of a pseudo-democracy. *Spring Awakening* doesn't go into this problem. Perhaps the Masked Man takes Melchior to an ego-land of hedonistic daydreams. But perhaps his 'doubt of having everything' is more than a *fin de siècle* pose. It could be the understanding of the inter-relatedness of living things and events, an understanding that the place where he is, and the society in which he is, are *also* man.

People used to think they had a secret soul, a centre of introspection in which god had set his tent. It might seem that the world was absurd and immorality triumphant, but every man carried the divine order in his soul and at the end of time justice would be decided there. Soul was god. In the nineteenth century god died and the soul became an empty tomb, a hole you could fall into and be lost. There was no infinite justice, only the terror of nothingness; no meaning, everything was possible. Soul was now almost the devil. We have no use for these images of soul because we can't wait for the justice of another world. We can't tolerate the injustice of this one. But we need an image of ourselves that doesn't condemn us to egoism or the absurd. When we talk about self-knowledge or self-consciousness, when we consider the standard by which we judge ourselves and others, so that we can make sense of our lives, when we look into the hidden mirror — what do we see? Other faces. The most intimate part of man is the most public. When we're most near to ourselves we find other people. To use the language of earlier times: soul is other people. My soul lives in others — but remains mine. That shouldn't surprise us, we're social animals. But we have to understand that if we act towards others with a lower standard than our self-respect, so that our other-consciousness is inferior to our self-consciousness — then that lower standard is also a form of action or existence that we experience as part of ourselves, and must criticise by the very act of being self-conscious. Self-consciousness isn't merely intellectual, it's an emotional awareness of our right to justice and autonomy. It is the standard we have for ourselves, the judgement we make of ourselves. That is inalienable from self-consciousness. If we try to have two standards — one for ourselves and one for others — we *must* become self-critical, must live in conflict with ourselves. Then no matter how much we consume we are still feeding, clothing and entertaining someone we can't live with. This conflict is most acute in the authoritarian man. His mind and emotions are so well schooled in hate, that the only way he can live with the self-hatred that results is by sacrificing himself to the hero of destruction: the fascist leader.

Our education, social myths, economic activity, all develop this spirit. Our culture fouls the mirror and heaps trash on it. The class-divided consumer society can't solve this problem. We must remain as unsatisfied as beggars till we can act towards other people as we act towards ourselves, and till then we can't have a culture but only an organisation. An organisation is based on class-division. It can accommodate machines but not fulfil people or even satisfy them. That's why it's inefficient and self-destructive. Human beings must have a full culture in the sense I've described because, only when they live in co-operation, mutual respect and affability with their community, can they bear to live with themselves. Human discontent can only be satisfied by this sort of culture, or at least the knowledge that we're working for it. Our crisis isn't just about technology. It's a crisis of the species. We no longer know how to live or survive. The only way to begin to solve this crisis is to look in the mirror and see other people. Did the Masked Man lead Melchior to die in the First World War, going straight from spring to winter? Our future is as doubtful. We have to understand the dangers, the opportunities and the shortage of time. Time is no longer a benign old man with a white beard, a staff and a lantern. It is a crying child tugging at our sleeve and asking to be carried.

EDWARD BOND
1974

A Note on the Language

The English version is meant to be acted, and so I have simplified
the original German in a few places. An example is the opening of
the last scene. Melchior's description of the graveyard is more
elaborate in the German. To me it sounded a bit like a description
of a Walt Disney graveyard. If I had kept *all* the original
elaboration it would have been unspeakable by contemporary
performers. Performers at the turn of the century thought and
spoke in paragraphs. For better or worse, contemporary
performers think and speak — and their audiences think and
listen — in sentences. The architectural construction of paragraphs
sounds artificial to us. It has been destroyed by the wisecrack, the
retort, the exclamation. Nevertheless the language in this
translation remains elaborate and in places consciously literary.
That is because the characters use language and imagery in a more
complex way than most of us do. The performers must *use* this
complexity, and not try to sweep it under the carpet as a
nuisance. It is at the heart of the play. The characters are afraid
to use their bodies, and so their language becomes either an
embrace or a blow. It's easy to find examples of this — the judge's
verbal sadism is one. Many of the others have the same fault.
There is the children's imitation of their elders' clichés — because
these represent maturity for them. And Melchior's mother uses
style to lie to herself. How else can you describe her
extraordinary tendentiousness in her scene with Melchior and
Moritz? Later she masturbates herself with words in her letter to
Moritz; she uses morality like a coquette. And her argument with
the judge is a calculated intercourse between two rapists. When
her deceit is finally pierced the suddenness of the change shows
her emotional state. She is not slowly persuaded; it's as if her
husband suddenly knocked down a wall in her mind and revealed
another room already completely furnished and inhabited. She
immediately produces a few words as ruthless and cruel as
anyone's in the play.

None of the characters can describe the things that matter or could save them. The elders don't discuss, they make speeches. Their voices flatten silence like drums, and their tongues beat out the rhythms like wooden drum sticks. The exception to all this is the Masked Man. He is usually drier and more ironic. Wedekind called the play a comedy — and it is very funny. But almost all the intentional jokes are made by the Masked Man. The others are too afraid to laugh, and so they can't think.

EDWARD BOND
1974

Cast List

This translation of *Spring Awakening* was first staged on 24 May, 1974 at the National Theatre, with the following cast:

Children

MELCHIOR GABOR	Peter Firth
MORITZ STIEFEL	Michael Kitchen
HÄNSCHEN RILOW	Dai Bradley
ERNST RÖBEL	Gerard Ryder
OTTO	David Dixon
GEORG ZIRSCHNITZ	Keith Skinner
ROBERT	Martin Howells
LÄMMERMEIER,	Christopher Guard
WENDLA BERGMANN	Veronica Quilligan
MARTHA BESSEL	Jane Carr
THEA	Jenny Agutter
ILSE	Patti Love

Boys in the Reformatory

DIETER	Rupert Frazer
REINHOLD	Ian Mackenzie
RUPERT	James Smith
HELMUT	Glyn Grain
GASTON	Bryan Brown

Parents

HERR GABOR	Joseph O'Conor
HERR STIEFEL	James Mellor
FRAU GABOR	Susan Engel
FRAU BERGMANN	Beryl Reid
INA MÜLLER, Wendla's sister	Judith Paris

Teachers

HEADMASTER SUNSTROKE	William Squire

PROFESSOR GUTGRINDER	Kenneth Benda
PROFESSOR BONEBREAKER	Alex McCrindle
PROFESSOR TONGUETWISTER	Stephen Williams
PROFESSOR FLYSWATTER	Peter Needham
PROFESSOR THICKSTICK	Kenneth Mackintosh
PROFESSOR APELARD	Colin Fay

Other adults

THE MASKED MAN	Cyril Cusack
DR LEMONADE	Daniel Thorndike
DR PROCRUSTES	Alan Hay
REVEREND BALDBELLY	Pitt Wilkinson
FASTCRAWLER, the school porter	Alan Hay
FRIEND ZIEG (named GOAT in this text)	Glyn Grain
LOCKSMITH	Pitt Wilkinson
UNCLE PROBST	Peter Rocca

Directed by Bill Bryden

The action takes place in a provincial town in Germany, 1891-1892.

Act One

SCENE ONE

Living room.

WENDLA. Why have you made my dress so long, mother?

FRAU BERGMANN. You're fourteen today.

WENDLA. I'd rather not have been fourteen if I'd known you'd make my dress so long.

FRAU BERGMANN. Your dress isn't too long, Wendla. What next? Can I help it if my child is four inches taller every spring? A grown girl can't still go round dressed like a little princess.

WENDLA. At least the little princess's dress suits me better than this nightshirt. Let me wear it once more, mother. One more long summer. Fourteen or fifteen, that's still soon enough for this sackcloth. Let's keep it till my next birthday. I'd only trip over the braid and tear it.

FRAU BERGMANN. I don't know what I should say. I'd willingly keep you exactly as you are, darling. Other girls are stringy or plump at your age. You're not. Who knows what you'll be like when they're grown up?

WENDLA. Who knows — perhaps I won't be anything anymore.

FRAU BERGMANN. Child, child, where d'you get these ideas?

WENDLA. Don't, mummy. Don't be sad.

FRAU BERGMANN (*kisses her*). My precious.

WENDLA. They come to me in the evening when I can't sleep. It doesn't make me the least bit sad, and I go to sleep better then. Is it a sin to think about such things, mother?

FRAU BERGMANN. Go and hang the sackcloth in the wardrobe. Put your little princess's dress on again and God bless you. When I get a moment I'll sew a broad flounce round the bottom.

WENDLA (*hanging the dress in the wardrobe*). No, I'd rather even be twenty than that . . .!

FRAU BERGMANN. Only so that you don't catch cold! There was a time when this little dress was too long on you, but . . .

WENDLA. Now, when summer's coming? O mother, even children don't catch diptheria in the knees! How can you be so fussy? You don't feel cold when you're my age — least of all in your knees. Would it be better if I was too hot? You ought to thank God that early one morning your precious doesn't rip the sleeves off her dress and come to you before it's still light with no shoes and stockings on! When I wear my sackcloth I'll be dressed like a fairy queen underneath. Don't be cross, mummy. No one can see it then.

SCENE TWO

Sunday evening.

MELCHIOR. It's too boring. I give up.

OTTO. Then we'll all have to stop! — Have you done your homework, Melchior?

MELCHIOR. Go on playing!

MORITZ. Where are you going?

MELCHIOR. Walking.

GEORG. It'll be dark soon!

ROBERT. Have you done your homework already?

MELCHIOR. Why shouldn't I walk in the dark?

ERNST. Central America! Louis the fifteenth! Sixty verses of Homer! Seven quadratic equations!

MELCHIOR. Damned homework!

GEORG. If only the Latin essay wasn't wanted tomorrow!

MORITZ. You can't think of anything without homework getting in the way!

OTTO. I'm going home.

GEORG. And me. Homework!

ERNST. And me, and me.

ROBERT. 'Night, Melchior.

MELCHIOR. Sleep well!

They all go except MORITZ and MELCHIOR.

MELCHIOR. I'd like to know exactly what we're in this world
   for!
MORITZ. School makes me wish I was a cart horse! What do we
   go to school for? To be examined! And why are we examined?
   So we can fail. Seven have got to fail because the next class is
   only big enough for sixty. — I've felt so odd since Christmas
   . . . O hell, if it wasn't for papa I'd pack my things tonight and
   sign on board a ship.
MELCHIOR. Let's talk about something else.

   They walk.

MORITZ. Look at that cat with its tail poking up in the air!
MELCHIOR. D'you believe in omens?
MORITZ. Don't really know. It came from over there. It's
   nothing.
MELCHIOR. In my opinion that's the Charybdis people fall into
   when they try to rise out of the Scylla of religious superstition.
   Let's sit under this beech. The warm wind's blowing over the
   mountains. I'd like to be a little animal that's rocked and
   swayed in the tops of the trees the whole night.
MORITZ. Undo your waistcoat, Melchior.
MELCHIOR. O, the way the wind blows your clothes!
MORITZ. God, it's getting pitch dark, you can't see a hand stuck
   up in front of you. Where are you, actually? — Melchior, don't
   you also think that man's sense of shame is just a product of
   his education?
MELCHIOR. I was thinking about that the other day. It seems to
   me, at least, it's deeply rooted in human nature. For example,
   suppose you had to completely strip off in front of your best
   friend. You wouldn't do it, not unless he does it at the same
   time. — But then perhaps it's all just a question of whatever
   happens to be in good taste.
MORITZ. I've already decided when I have children I'll let them
   sleep together in the same room, in the same bed if possible —
   boys and girls. I'll let them help each other to dress and
   undress morning and night, and when it's hot the boys and
   the girls will both wear nothing all day except a white wollen
   tunic and a leather belt. I think that then when they grow up
   they won't be as tense as most of us are.

MELCHIOR. I'm sure of it! The only question is, what about when the girls have babies?

MORITZ. Why have babies?

MELCHIOR. I believe in a definite instinct in these things. For example, suppose you keep two cats — a tom and a bitch — shut up together from when they're kittens. You keep them away from all contact with the outside world so they've only got their instincts left. Sooner or later the cat will become pregnant, even though they had no example to follow.

MORITZ. With animals that must finally happen by itself.

MELCHIOR. Even more so with men I think! Listen, Moritz, when your boys are sleeping in the same bed with your girls and suddenly they feel their first masculine itch — I'll take a bet with anyone that —

MORITZ. You may be right. But still.

MELCHIOR. And I'm sure it would be just the same with the girls! Not that girls actually — obviously one can't speak definitely — but at least you can surmise — and their natural curiosity would do the rest!

MORITZ. By the way, I've got a question.

MELCHIOR. What?

MORITZ. But you will answer?

MELCHIOR. Of course!

MORITZ. Promise!

MELCHIOR. My hand on it. Well, Moritz?

MORITZ. Have you really done your homework?

MELCHIOR. Come on, you can tell me. There's no one else here.

MORITZ. Of course, my children will have to work all day in the farm or the garden — or play games that are good for their bodies. Riding, gymnastics, climbing — and certainly no sleeping on soft beds like us. We're terribly weak. I don't believe you'd ever have dreams if you slept on a hard bed.

MELCHIOR. From now till after the harvest I'm only going to sleep in my hammock. I've put my bed away. It folds up . . . Last winter I dreamed I whipped our Rufus so long he couldn't move. That's the worst thing I've dreamed. — Why are you staring at me like that?

MORITZ. Have you already felt it?

MELCHIOR. What?

MORITZ. How you said.

MELCHIOR. The masculine itch?

MORITZ. H-hm.

MELCHIOR. And how!

MORITZ. Me too.

MELCHIOR. I've been able to for a long time. Almost a year now.

MORITZ. It was like being struck by lightning.

MELCHIOR. Did you have a dream?

MORITZ. But only very short — some legs in bright blue ballet tights climbing over the teacher's desk or at any rate I thought they wanted to climb over — I only caught a glimpse.

MELCHIOR. Georg Zirnschnitz dreamed about his *mother*!

MORITZ. Did he tell you that?

MELCHIOR. Out on Hangman's Hill.

MORITZ. If you knew what I've gone through since that night!

MELCHIOR. Bad conscience?

MORITZ. Bad conscience? *Fear of death*!

MELCHIOR. My God!

MORITZ. I thought I was incurable. I believed I was suffering from an internal defect. In the end I only quietened down when I started to write my Memoirs. Yes, yes, Melchior, the last three weeks have been a Golgotha to me.

MELCHIOR. I was more or less all set for it. I felt a bit ashamed. But that was all.

MORITZ. And you're almost a whole year younger than me!

MELCHIOR. I shouldn't give it another thought, Moritz. In my experience there isn't a set age for the first time these feelings turn up. You know that tall Lammermeier with the blond hair and hooked nose? He's three years older than me. Hänschen Rilow says he still dreams about apple tart and custard.

MORITZ. Chuck it, Melchior, how can Hänschen Rilow know?

MELCHIOR. He asked him.

MORITZ. He asked him? I wouldn't dare ask anyone.

MELCHIOR. You just asked me.

MORITZ. Good Lord, yes! Perhaps Hänschen also wrote his Last Will! The games they play with us! And we're supposed to be grateful. I don't remember ever wanting that sort of excitement! Why couldn't I just sleep in peace till it was all over? My poor parents could have had a hundred better children than me. But I came, I don't know how, and then it's my fault I didn't stay away! Haven't you ever thought about that, Melchior, exactly how we came into this madhouse?

MELCHIOR. You don't even know that, Moritz?

MORITZ. How should I! I see how hens lay eggs, and I hear mother's supposed to have carried me under her heart! Is that enough? And I remember that when I was five I was already embarrassed when anyone turned up the Queen of Hearts with the low-cut dress. That feeling's gone. But now I can't even speak to a girl without something I ought to be ashamed of coming into my head and — I swear to you, Melchior — I don't know *what*.

MELCHIOR. I'll tell you everything. I got it partly from books, partly from illustrations, partly from looking at nature. You'll be surprised. It turned me into an atheist. I've already told Georg Zirnschnitz! He wanted to tell Hänschen Rilow, but he'd already had it from his governess when he was a kid.

MORITZ. I've gone through the encyclopaedia from A to Z. Words — nothing but words, words! Not one single straight-forward explanation. O this feeling of shame! What good is an encyclopaedia if it doesn't answer the first questions about life?

MELCHIOR. Have you ever seen two dogs running across the street?

MORITZ. No! You'd better not tell me now, Melchior. I've got to face Central America and Louis the fifteenth! As well as sixty verses of Homer, seven quadratic equations, the Latin essay — I'd just get into hot water with everyone again tomorrow. When you have to study like a cart horse you must be as docile and stupid as a donkey.

MELCHIOR. Come back to my room. In three quarters of an hour I'll do the Homer, the equations, and *two* essays. I'll decorate yours with a few simple mistakes, and the ball's in the hole! Mother will make us some more lemonade and we'll have a pleasant chat about reproduction.

MORITZ. I can't. I can't have a pleasant chat about reproduction. If you want to do me a favour give me some written instructions. Write down all you know. Write it as simply and clearly as possible and stick it in my book during PT tomorrow. I'll take it home without knowing it's there. I'll come across it sometime when I'm not expecting to. I won't be able to stop my weary eyes running over it . . . If it's absolutely unavoidable you can go as far as a few diagrams in the margin.

MELCHIOR. You're like a girl. Well, have it your own way! It'll be rather interesting homework. One thing, Moritz.

MORITZ. Hn?

MELCHIOR. Have you seen a girl?

MORITZ. Yes!

MELCHIOR. Everything?

MORITZ. The lot.

MELCHIOR. And me! So you won't need many diagrams.

MORITZ. At the fair. In the cubicle at the back of the wax works. If I'd been caught I'd have been chased out of school! So beautiful — and o! as clear as daylight.

MELCHIOR. Last summer I was with mama at Frankfurt . . . Are you going already, Moritz?

MORITZ. Homework. 'Night.

MELCHIOR. Good night.

SCENE THREE

THEA, WENDLA *and* MARTHA *come along the street arm in arm.*

MARTHA. How the water gets into your shoes!

WENDLA. How the wind blows in your face!

THEA. How your heart thumps!

WENDLA. Let's go to the bridge. Ilse said the river's full of trees and bushes. The boys have taken a raft out on the water. They say Melchior Gabor was nearly drowned last night.

THEA. O, he can swim!

MARTHA. Of course he can, brat!

WENDLA. If he couldn't swim he could easily have been drowned!

THEA. Your plait's coming undone, Martha! Your plait's coming undone!

MARTHA. O — let it come undone! It annoys me day and night.
I mustn't have short hair like you, I mustn't have natural hair
like Wendla, I mustn't have a fringe, I even have to go round
the house with it done up — all to please my aunts!

WENDLA. Tomorrow I'll bring some scissors to Bible class. While
you recite "Blessed is the man who walks not in the counsel of
the wicked" I'll cut it off.

MARTHA. For God's sake, Wendla! Papa beats me till I'm
crippled and mama locks me up in the coal cellar for three
nights at a time.

WENDLA. What does he beat you with, Martha?

MARTHA. Sometimes I think they'd miss something if they
didn't have a disgraceful brat like me!

THEA. But, Martha!

WENDLA. And they wouldn't let you thread a bright blue ribbon
through the top of your petticoat like us?

THEA. Pink satin! Mama insists pink satin goes with my pitch
black eyes.

MARTHA. Blue looked so well on me! Mama pulled me out of
my bed by my plait. Well — I fell head first flat on the floor.
You see, mother comes up to pray with us every evening . . .

WENDLA. If I was you I'd have run far away long ago.

MARTHA. "There you are, see what it'll come to! Yes, there you
are! But she'll learn — O, she'll soon learn! At least I'll never
be able to blame my mother when anything goes wrong —"

THEA. Hoo hoo!

MARTHA. D'you know what my mother meant by that, Thea?

THEA. No. Do you, Wendla?

WENDLA. I'd have asked her.

MARTHA. I lay on the floor and screamed and roared. Then
papa comes. Rip — petticoat down. I'm out through the door.
"There you are! Now I want to go out on the street like
that! —"

WENDLA. But that wasn't true, Martha!

MARTHA. I was freezing. I'd got the street door open. I had to
sleep in a sack all night.

THEA. I couldn't sleep in a sack to save my life!

WENDLA. I'd like to sleep in your sack for you once.

MARTHA. If only they wouldn't beat me.

THEA. But you'd suffocate in it!

MARTHA. Your head's free. They tie it under your chin.

THEA. And then they beat you?

MARTHA. No. Only when it's something special.

WENDLA. What do they beat you with, Martha?

MARTHA. O, whatever they lay their hands on. Does *your* mother maintain it's indecent to eat bread in bed?

WENDLA. No, no.

MARTHA. I always think, they have their pleasure — even though they never talk about it. When I have children I'll let them grow up like the weeds in our rose garden. No one looks after them but they grow tall and strong — and the roses get weaker every summer and hang down on their stems.

THEA. When I have children I'll dress them all in pink — pink hats, little pink dresses, pink shoes. Only the stockings — stockings pitch black. When I go for a walk I'll let them all trot along in front of me. What about you, Wendla?

WENDLA. D'you already know you'll get some?

THEA. Why shouldn't we get some?

MARTHA. Aunt Euphemia hasn't got any.

THEA. Goose! Because she's not *married*!

WENDLA. Aunt Bauer was married three times — and she hasn't got even one.

MARTHA. If you do get some, Wendla, what d'you want: boys or girls?

WENDLA. Boys! Boys!

THEA. And boys for me!

MARTHA. And me. I'd rather have twenty boys than three girls.

THEA. Girls are boring.

MARTHA. If I wasn't already a girl I know I wouldn't want to become one.

WENDLA. That's a matter of taste, Martha. I'm happy because I'm a girl. Believe me I wouldn't change places with a king's son. — But I still only want boys!

THEA. That's stupid, so stupid, Wendla!

WENDLA. But surely, child, it must be a thousand times more ennobling to be loved by a man than a girl!

THEA. You're not claiming that Herr Pfalle the Junior Afforestation Officer loves Melli more than she loves him?

WENDLA. Of course I do, Thea. Pfalle has pride. He's proud of being a Junior Afforestation Officer — because that's all he's got! But Melli has *bliss* — because she's got a million times more than she had when she was on her own!

MARTHA. Aren't you proud of yourself, Wendla?

WENDLA. That would be silly.

THEA. Watch how she walks — how she looks — how she holds herself, Martha! If that's not pride!

WENDLA. But why? I'm just so happy at being a girl. If I wasn't a girl I'd kill myself so that next time . . .

MELCHIOR *passes and greets them.*

THEA. He's got such a wonderful head.

MARTHA. He makes me think of the young Alexander going to school with Aristotle.

THEA. O God, Greek history! All I remember is that Socrates lay in a barrel while Alexander sold him a donkey's shadow.

WENDLA. I heard he's third in his class.

THEA. Professor Bonebreaker says he could be first if he wanted.

MARTHA. He's got a beautiful forehead, but his friend's got soulful eyes.

THEA. Moritz Stiefel? That doormouse, always asleep.

MARTHA. I've always found him very interesting company.

THEA. He puts you in a compromising situation everytime you meet. At the Rilow's Children's Ball he offered me some chocolates. Imagine, Wendla, they were warm and soft. Isn't that — ? He said they'd been in his trousers too long.

WENDLA. What d'you think: Melchior Gabor once told me he didn't believe in anything — not in God, the afterworld— hardly in anything in this world!

SCENE FOUR

Park in front of the Grammar School.

MELCHIOR, OTTO, GEORG, ROBERT, HÄNSCHEN RILOW, LAMMERMEIER.

MELCHIOR. D'you know where Moritz Stiefel's got to?

GEORG. He'll catch it! O, he'll catch it!

OTTO. He goes too far, he'll trip up one day!

LAMMERMEIER. God knows I wouldn't like to be in his shoes now!

ROBERT. Impertinence! Disgraceful!

MELCHIOR. What — what is it?

GEORG. What is it? I'll tell you what it is . . .

LAMMERMEIER. I don't want to be involved.

OTTO. Nor me — God, no.

MELCHIOR. If you don't tell me immediately . . .

ROBERT. It's very simple, Moritz Stiefel is burglaring the staff room.

MELCHIOR. The staff room!

OTTO. The staff room. Straight after Latin.

GEORG. He was last. He stayed behind on purpose.

LAMMERMEIER. When I went down the corridor I saw him open the door.

MELCHIOR. I'll be damned!

LAMMERMEIER. No — he'll be!

GEORG. They probably forgot the key.

ROBERT. Or Moritz carries a skeleton key.

OTTO. I wouldn't put that past him!

LAMMERMEIER. He'll be lucky if all he gets is detention.

ROBERT. It'll go on his report.

OTTO. If the governors don't just kick him out.

HÄNSCHEN. There he is.

MELCHIOR. White as a sheet.

MORITZ *comes in in frantic excitement.*

LAMMERMEIER. Moritz, Moritz, what have you done now!

MORITZ. Nothing — nothing . . .

ROBERT. You're shaking.

MORITZ. With excitement — with happiness —with luck.

OTTO. Were you copped?

MORITZ. I've passed! Melchior, I've passed! O now the world can go to hell! I've passed! Who thought I'd pass? I still can't believe it! I read it twenty times! I couldn't believe it! O God it was still there! Still there! *I've passed!* (*Smiles.*) I don't know — it's so funny — the floor's going round — Melchior,

Melchior, if you knew what it was like!

HÄNSCHEN. Congratulations, Moritz. Just be grateful you got away.

MORITZ. You can't know, Hänschen, you can't imagine the risk! For three weeks I crept by that door as if it was the gates of hell. And today a crack, the door was open. I think if someone had offered me a fortune — nothing, o nothing could have stopped me! I stood in the middle of the room. I pulled the files open — tore through the pages — there it is! — and the whole time . . . I'm shuddering.

MELCHIOR. And the whole time . . .?

MORITZ. The whole time the door was wide open behind me. How I got out — how I got down the stairs I'll never know.

HÄNSCHEN. Has Ernst Röbel passed?

MORITZ. O yes, Hänschen! Ernst Röbel passed too!

ROBERT. Then you didn't read it right. If you don't count the dunces, then we and you and Röbel make sixty-one, and the next class only holds sixty.

MORITZ. I read it perfectly clearly. Ernst Röbel goes up as well as me — of course at the moment we're both only provisional. Next term they'll decide which of us has to give way. Poor Röbel! God knows I'm not worried about myself now. I've been too near the abyss already.

OTTO. I bet five marks you have to give way.

MORITZ. You haven't got it. I don't want to clean you out. O Lord, I'll work like a slave after this. I can tell you now — I don't care if you believe me — it doesn't matter anymore — I — I know how true it is: if I hadn't passed I'd have shot myself.

ROBERT. With a peashooter!

GEORG. Yellow belly!

OTTO. I'd like to see you shoot!

LAMMERMEIER. Clip his ear and see what he does!

MELCHIOR (*hits* LAMMERMEIER). Come on, Moritz. Let's go to the forester's hut.

GEORG. You don't believe that rubbish!

MELCHIOR. Would it bother you? Let them chatter, Moritz, we'll go — out of this town!

PROFESSORS GUTGRINDER *and* BONEBREAKER *go by*.

BONEBREAKER. Beyond my comprehension, my dear fellow, how my best student can feel himself drawn towards precisely my very worst.

GUTGRINDER. Beyond mine too, my dear chap.

SCENE FIVE

A sunny afternoon.

MELCHIOR *and* WENDLA *meet each other in the forest.*

MELCHIOR. Is it really you, Wendla? What are you doing up here on your own? I've been wandering through the forest for three hours without meeting a soul, and now suddenly you come towards me out of the trees.

WENDLA. Yes, it's me.

MELCHIOR. If I didn't know you were Wendla Bergmann I'd think you were a wood nymph that's fallen out of the branches.

WENDLA. No, no, I'm Wendla Bergmann. Where have you come from?

MELCHIOR. I've been thinking.

WENDLA. I'm collecting woodruff. Mama uses them for spring wine. She *was* coming with me but Aunt Bauer turned up at the last moment. She doesn't like climbing so I came on my own.

MELCHIOR. Have you got the woodruff?

WENDLA. A whole basket full! It's as thick as clover over there under the beeches. Now I'm trying to find a path. I seem to have gone wrong. Perhaps you could tell me what time it is?

MELCHIOR. Just after half past three. When are you expected?

WENDLA. I thought it was later. I lay down quite a while on the moss by the stream and dreamed. Time went so quickly. I was afraid evening was already coming.

MELCHIOR. If you're not expected, let's stay here a little bit longer. My favourite spot's under the oak. If you lean your head back against the trunk and stare through the branches up at the sky, it hypnotises you. The ground's still warm from the sun this morning. — I've wanted to ask you something for weeks, Wendla.

WENDLA. But I must be home by five.

MELCHIOR. We'll go together. I'll carry the basket and we'll go along the river bed and be on the bridge in ten minutes. When you lie like this with your head propped in your hands you have the strangest ideas . . .

Both are lying under the oak.

WENDLA. What did you want to ask me, Melchior?

MELCHIOR. I know you often visit the poor, Wendla, and take them food and clothes and money. D'you go because you want to or does your mother send you?

WENDLA. Mostly mother sends me. They're poor working-class families with too many children. Often the man can't find work so they're cold and hungry. We've got a lot of left-over things lying about in cupboards and drawers, we'll never use them now. What made you think of that?

MELCHIOR. Are you pleased when your mother sends you?

WENDLA. O very pleased! How can you ask!

MELCHIOR. But the children are dirty, the women are sick, the rooms are crowded with filth, the men hate you because you don't have to work . . .

WENDLA. That's not true, Melchior. And if it were true I'd go even more.

MELCHIOR. Why even more, Wendla?

WENDLA. I'd go to them even more. It would give me far more happiness to be able to help them.

MELCHIOR. So you go to the poor to make yourself happy?

WENDLA. I go to them because they're poor.

MELCHIOR. And if it didn't make you happy you wouldn't go?

WENDLA. Can I help it if it makes me happy?

MELCHIOR. And for that you go to heaven! I was right, I've been going over this for a month! Can a miser help it if visiting dirty, sick children doesn't make him happy?

WENDLA. O, I'm sure it would make you very happy!

MELCHIOR. And yet because of that he suffers eternal damnation! I'll write an essay and send it to the Reverend Baldbelly. He put all this in my head! Why does he drivel on at us about the joys of sacrificing yourself for others? If he can't answer, I'm not going to any more confirmation classes and I won't be confirmed.

WENDLA. Don't make your poor parents miserable over that! Let them confirm you. They don't cut your head off. If it wasn't for our dreadful white dresses and your baggy trousers we might even get some fun out of it.

MELCHIOR. There is no self-sacrifice! There is no selflessness! I watch the good enjoying themselves while the bad tremble and groan — I watch you shaking your curls and laughing, Wendla Bergmann, and it all makes me feel as lost as an outcast — Wendla, what did you dream about when you were on the grass by the stream?

WENDLA. Nonsense — silly things . . .

MELCHIOR. With your eyes open?

WENDLA. I dreamed I was a poor, poor beggar girl. I was sent out on the streets every morning before five. I had to beg from brutal, heartless people, all day in the storm and rain. And when I came home at night, shivering with hunger and cold, and when I didn't have all the money my father wanted, I was beaten . . . beaten . . .

MELCHIOR. I understand, Wendla. You get that from silly children's books. I promise you there aren't brutal people like that any more.

WENDLA. O no, Melchior, you're wrong. Martha Bessel is beaten night after night and you can see the weals next day. O what she must suffer! It makes me hot when she tells us about it. I pity her so much. I often have to cry in my pillow in the middle of the night. I've been thinking for months how I can help her. I'd happily take her place just for one week.

MELCHIOR. The father should be reported immediately. Then they'd take the child away.

WENDLA. I haven't been hit in my whole life, Melchior — not even once. I can hardly imagine what it's like to be beaten. I've beaten myself to find out what it does to you. It must be a horrifying feeling.

MELCHIOR. I don't believe it ever makes a child better.

WENDLA. What?

MELCHIOR. Being beaten.

WENDLA. With this switch for example. Ugh, how springy and thin.

MELCHIOR. That would draw blood.

WENDLA. Would you like to beat me with it once?

MELCHIOR. Who?

WENDLA. Me.

MELCHIOR. What's the matter, Wendla?

WENDLA. There's no harm in it.

MELCHIOR. O be quiet! I won't beat you.

WENDLA. But if I let you do it!

MELCHIOR. No, Wendla.

WENDLA. But if I ask you for it, Melchior!

MELCHIOR. Are you out of your mind?

WENDLA. I've never been beaten in my whole life!

MELCHIOR. If you can ask for something like that . . .

WENDLA. Please, please!

MELCHIOR. I'll teach you to ask! (*He hits her.*)

WENDLA. O God — I don't feel it at all . . .

MELCHIOR. Of course not — through all your skirts.

WENDLA. Then beat my legs!

MELCHIOR. Wendla! (*He hits her harder.*)

WENDLA. You're only stroking me! Stroking me!

MELCHIOR. You wait, you bitch, I'll thrash the hide off you!

> *He throws the stick away and hits out at her with his fists. She bursts into a terrible scream. He takes no notice and punches at her in fury. Heavy tears stream down his face. He jumps up, grips his head and runs into the wood sobbing with misery.*

Act Two

SCENE ONE

Evening in Melchior's study.

The window is open, the lamp burns on the table. MELCHIOR *and* MORITZ *sit on the sofa.*

MORITZ. I'm quite lively again now, just a bit on edge. But I slept all through Greek. I'm surprised old Tonguetwister didn't twist my ears. I just scraped in on time this morning. My first thought when I woke up was irregular verbs. Damnation-hell-and-fireworks, I conjugated all through breakfast and all the way to school, till everything was green in front of my eyes . . . I must have gone blank about three. The pen made one more blot in my book. When Mathilde woke me up the lamp was smoking and the blackbirds were singing their hearts out in the lilac under the window — suddenly I felt so completely miserable again. I fastened my collar and put a brush through my hair. — But you feel satisfied when you've forced something out of yourself.
MELCHIOR. May I roll you a cigarette?
MORITZ. Thanks, I'm not smoking. — If I can only keep it up! I'll work and work till my eyes drop out. Ernst Röbel's already failed six times since the holidays: three times in Greek, twice with Bonebreaker, the last time in literary history. I've only been in that pitiful condition five times, and and it's definitely not happening again! Röbel won't shoot himself! Röbel's parents didn't sacrifice everything for him. He can become a mercenary whenever he likes, or a cowboy or a sailor. If *I* fail my father will have a heart attack and my mother go into a madhouse. I'd never survive it. Before the exams I prayed like Christ in the garden, I implored God to let me catch consumption so that this bitter cup would pass. It passed — but I'm still afraid to look up day or night. The

halo that floats over it is winking at me from the distance. Well now I've got the bull by the horns I'm going to climb on its back. Then if I fall I have an infallible guarantee that I'll break my neck.

MELCHIOR. Life is always unexpectedly mean. I rather incline to hanging myself from a tree. What's keeping mama with the tea?

MORITZ. Tea will do me good. I'm actually shaking, Melchior! I feel so strangely disembodied. Please touch me. I see — I hear — I feel much more clearly — and yet it's all in a dream — o, so strange. The garden's lying down there in the moonlight, so still and deep, as if it's lying in eternity. There are veiled figures coming out of the ground under the bushes. They hurry over the clearings — busy and breathless — and vanish in the dusk. It's as if a meeting's gathering under the chestnut trees. Shouldn't we go down, Melchior?

MELCHIOR. After tea.

MORITZ. The leaves are rustling like little insects! It's as if my dead grandmother was telling me the story of "The Queen with No Head". There was a beautiful queen, as beautiful as the sun, more beautiful than all the other girls. But unfortunately she came into the world with no head. She couldn't eat, or drink, or see, or laugh, or even kiss. She could only make the court understand her by her soft little hands, and she tapped out declarations of war and death sentences with her pretty little feet. One day she was defeated by a king who happened to have two heads. They got in each other's hair all the time and quarrelled so much that neither of them could get a word in. The top wizard took the smaller head and put it on the queen. There, it fits marvellously. So the king married the queen, and instead of getting in each other's hair they kissed: on their foreheads, their cheeks, their mouths — and lived happily ever after. All rubbish! Since the holidays I can't get the headless queen out of my mind. When I see a beautiful girl, I see her with no head — and I keep suddenly seeing myself with no head . . . Perhaps one day someone will put a head on me.

    FRAU GABOR *brings tea and puts it on the table in front of* MORITZ *and* MELCHIOR.

FRAU GABOR. There, boys, drink your tea. Good evening, Herr
    Stiefel, how are you?

MORITZ. Thank you, Frau Gabor. — I'm watching the dance
    down there.

FRAU GABOR. You don't look too well. D'you feel all right?

MORITZ. It's nothing. I've been going to bed a bit late the last
    few nights.

MELCHIOR. Imagine, he worked through the whole night.

FRAU GABOR. You shouldn't, Herr Stiefel. You must look after
    yourself. Think of your health. School can't give you your
    health back again. Brisk walks in the fresh air. That's worth
    more at your age than perfect grammar.

MORITZ. Yes — brisk walks! While you're walking you can work
    in your head! Why didn't I think of that? — But I'd still have
    to do the written work indoors.

MELCHIOR. Do the written stuff with me. That'll make it
    easier for both of us. Mother, you know Max von Trenk
    went down with nervous exhaustion? Well, Hänschen Rilow
    came straight from Trenk's deathbed lunch-time today and
    told the Head Trenk had just died in his presence. The Head
    said "Indeed. Haven't you still got two hours detention owing
    from last week? Here's a note for your Form Master. Get it
    sorted out. The whole class will assist at his funeral".
    Hänschen could hardly move.

FRAU GABOR. What's your book, Melchior?

MELCHIOR. *Faust.*

FRAU GABOR. Have you read it?

MELCHIOR. Not all of it.

MORITZ. We're just in the Walpurgis Night.

FRAU GABOR. If I were you I'd have waited a year or two for
    that.

MELCHIOR. I haven't come across any other book that I think is
    so beautiful, mother. Why shouldn't I read it?

FRAU GABOR. Because you don't understand it.

MELCHIOR. You can't know that, mother. Of course, I know I
    don't understand its deepest meaning . . .

MORITZ. We always read together. That makes it incredibly
    easier to understand.

FRAU GABOR. You're old enough to know what's good for

you and what's bad for you, Melchior. Do whatever you feel able to answer for to your own conscience. I shall be the first to acknowledge it if you never give me any cause to forbid you anything. I only want to make you aware that even the best can work harm when one lacks the maturity to know how to use it. But I shall always put my trust in you, rather than in some vague doctrine of education. If you need anything else, boys, come and call me, Melchior. I'm in my bedroom. *(Goes.)*

MORITZ. Your mother meant the business with Gretchen and the baby.

MELCHIOR. Did we even pause over it?

MORITZ. *Faust* couldn't have treated it more cold-bloodedly!

MELCHIOR. A common little scandal like that can't be the summit of such a masterpiece! Suppose Faust had just promised to marry her and then walked off? That would have been just as bad. There'd have been no baby — but Gretchen could still have died of a broken heart. When you see how frantically they all pounce on that one incident you'd think the whole world revolved round penis and vagina.

MORITZ. Frankly, Melchior, since reading your essay I feel it does. It fell out on the floor when I was reading a history book. I bolted the door and went through your lines like an owl flying through a burning wood. I think I read most of it with my eyes shut. It was like listening to your own forgotten memories — a song you hummed to yourself when you played as a child, and then hearing it again when you're lying down to die, coming out of someone else's mouth and breaking your heart. What moved me most was the part you wrote about the girl. I can't get it out of my mind. Honestly, Melchior, I'd rather suffer wrong than do wrong. To have to be over-powered by such a gentle force, and still be innocent — that seems the greatest sort of happiness to me.

MELCHIOR. I don't want to be given happiness like a beggar!

MORITZ. Why not?

MELCHIOR. I don't want anything I didn't have to fight for!

MORITZ. But would that still be happiness, Melchior? Melchior, the girl enjoys it like someone in heaven. It's a girl's nature to protect herself, to keep herself free from all bitterness till the last moment — so that she can feel all heaven falling on her at

once. A girl is afraid of hell even at the moment she steps into
paradise. Her feelings are as fresh as a stream when it breaks
from the rocks. The girl lifts up a chalice that no earthly
mouth has touched, a cup of flaming sparkling nectar and
gulps it down — I think the satisfaction a man gets out of it
must be cold and flat.

MELCHIOR. Think what you like but shut up. I don't like to
think about it . . .

SCENE TWO

FRAU BERGMANN *wearing a hat and cape, and with a beaming face,
comes through the middle door. She carries a basket on her arm.*

FRAU BERGMANN. Wendla! Wendla!

> WENDLA *appears in petticoat and stays at the side door
> right.*

WENDLA. What is it, mother?

FRAU BERGMANN. You're up already, precious? What a good
girl!

WENDLA. You've been out this early?

FRAU BERGMANN. Get dressed quickly. You must go down to
Ina. You must take her this basket.

WENDLA *(gets fully dressed during the following).* You've been
to Ina's? How was Ina? Won't she ever get better?

FRAU BERGMANN. You'll never guess, Wendla, last night the
stork was with her and brought her a little boy.

WENDLA. A boy! A boy! O that's wonderful! That's what her
chronic influenza was!

FRAU BERGMANN. A perfect boy!

WENDLA. I must see him, mother! Now I'm an aunt three times
— aunt to one girl and two boys!

FRAU BERGMANN. And what boys! That's what happens when
you live so close to the stork! It's only two years since she
walked up the aisle in her white dress.

WENDLA. Were you there when he brought him?

FRAU BERGMANN. He'd just flown off again. Don't you want

to pin on a rose?

WENDLA. Why didn't you get there a bit sooner, mother?

FRAU BERGMANN. I believe he might have brought you something too — a brooch perhaps.

WENDLA. It's such a pity.

FRAU BERGMANN. Now I told you he brought you a brooch.

WENDLA. I've got enough brooches.

FRAU BERGMANN. Then be contented, child. What more do you want?

WENDLA. I would very much like to have known whether he flew in through the window or down the chimney.

FRAU BERGMANN. You must ask Ina. O yes, you must ask Ina that, precious. Ina will tell you exactly. Ina spoke to him for a good half hour.

WENDLA. I shall ask Ina when I get there.

FRAU BERGMANN. And don't forget, precious. I shall be very interested myself to know if he came in through the window or the chimney.

WENDLA. Or perhaps I'd better ask the chimney-sweep. The chimney-sweep's bound to know if he used the chimney.

FRAU BERGMANN. Not the chimney-sweep, dear. Not the chimney-sweep. What does the chimney-sweep know about storks? He'll tell you all sorts of nonsense he doesn't believe himself. What — what are you staring at in the street?

WENDLA. Mother, a man — as big as three horses, with feet like paddle-steamers!

FRAU BERGMANN (*running to the window*). I don't believe it! I don't believe it!

WENDLA (*at the same time*). He's holding a bed-stead under his chin and playing "Watch on the Rhine" on it — he's just gone round the corner.

FRAU BERGMANN. You'll always be a child! Frightening your your silly old mother. Go and get your hat. I sometimes wonder if you'll ever get any sense in your head. I've given up hope.

WENDLA. So have I, mother, so have I. There's not much hope for my head. I've got a sister who's been married two and a half years, and I'm an aunt three times, and I've no idea how it all happens . . . Don't be cross, mummy, don't be cross!

Who in the world should I ask but you? Please, mummy, tell
me. Tell me, dear. I feel ashamed of myself. Do tell me,
mummy! Don't scold me for asking such things. Answer me —
what is it? — how does it happen? You can't really insist that
now I'm fourteen I still have to believe in the stork?

FRAU BERGMANN. But good lord, child, how funny you are!
What ideas you get! I really cannot do such a thing.

WENDLA. Why not, mother? Why not? It can't be anything ugly
if it makes you all so happy.

FRAU BERGMANN. O — O God help me! I would deserve to be
. . . Go and get dressed, Wendla. Get dressed.

WENDLA. I'll go . . . and what if your child goes to the chimney-
sweep to ask?

FRAU BERGMANN. But this will send me out of my mind!
Come here, Wendla, come to me. I'll tell you! I'll tell you
everything! O Almighty Father! — Only not now, Wendla.
Tomorrow, the day after tomorrow, next week — whenever
you like, my precious.

WENDLA. Tell me today, mother! Tell me now! This moment. I
can never stop asking now I've seen you so frightened.

FRAU BERGMANN. I can't Wendla.

WENDLA. O why can't you, Mummy? I'll kneel at your feet and
lay my head in your lap. Put your apron over my head and
talk and talk as if you were sitting alone in your room. I won't
flinch or cry out. I'll be patient and bear it whatever it is.

FRAU BERGMANN. Heaven knows none of this is my fault.
Wendla! Heaven sees into my heart. I'll put myself into God's
hands, Wendla — and tell you how you came into this world.
Now listen to me, Wendla.

WENDLA (*under the apron*). I'm listening.

FRAU BERGMANN (*ecstatically*). But I can't, child! I can't be
responsible! I'd deserve to be put in prison — to have you
taken away from me . . .

WENDLA (*under the apron*). Be brave, mother!

FRAU BERGMANN. Well, listen!

WENDLA (*under the apron, trembling*). O God, o God!

FRAU BERGMANN. To have a child — you understand me,
Wendla?

WENDLA. Quickly, mother — I can't bear it anymore.

FRAU BERGMANN. To have a child — the man — to whom
you're married — you must — *love* — love, you see — as you
can only love your husband. You must love him *very much
with your whole heart* — in a way that can't be put into words!
You must *love* him, Wendla, in a way that you certainly can't
love at your age . . . Now you know.

WENDLA *(getting up).* Well, good heavens!

FRAU BERGMANN. Now you know what a testing time lies
before you!

WENDLA. And that's all?

FRAU BERGMANN. As God is my witness! Now take that
basket and go to Ina. She'll give you some chocolate to drink,
and some cake too. Come on, let me look at you once more —
boots laced up, silk gloves, sailor suit, rose in your hair . . .
your little skirt really is getting too short for you, Wendla!

WENDLA. Have you bought the meat for lunch, mummy?

FRAU BERGMANN. God bless you. I must sew a broad flounce
round the bottom.

SCENE THREE

HANSCHEN RILOW *(with a light in his hand, he bolts the door
behind him and lifts the lid).* Have you prayed tonight
Desdemona?

> *He takes a reproduction of the Venus of Palma Vecchio
> from the inside pocket of his jacket.*

You don't look like the Lord's Prayer, darling — contemplating
the coming moments, the lovely moments of coming ecstasy
— still just as when I first saw you lying in the window of that
little corner shop, just as alluring with those smooth limbs,
this soft curve of the hips, these young, tense breasts — o, how
drunk the Great Master must have been when the fourteen-
year-old original lay stretched out before him on the studio
couch!

Will you come to me in my dreams now and then? I'll
welcome you with outstretched arms and kiss your breath

away. You'll take me over like an heiress moving back into her
deserted palace. Gates and doors fly open with unseen hands,
and down below in the park the fountain begins to splash
happily . . .
It is the cause! It is the cause! The terrible hammering in my
breast proves I'm not murdering you for a whim! My throat
goes dry when I think of the lonely nights ahead. And I swear
to you, woman, it's not the disgust that comes from over-
indulgence! Who'd flatter himself by being disgusted with
you? No — you suck the marrow from my bones, bend my
back, take the sparkle from my young eyes. Your inhuman
modesty is too demanding,'your motionless limbs too
exhausting! It's me or you! And I've won!
If I counted them all — all the others I fought this battle with
on this same spot! Ruben's Venus — bequeathed to me by
that waspish-thin governess Miss Hatherley-Brown, the rattle-
snake in my nursery paradise! Correggio's Io. Titian's Galathea.
J van Beer's Ada. Cupid by Bouguereau — the Cupid I
abducted from the secret drawer in papa's desk and locked up
in my harem. A quivering, trembling Leda by Makart I came
across in my brother's exercise books. *Seven*, o, lovely
candidate for death, have gone before you down the path to
Tartarus. Let that console you and don't make my torments
unbearable with those imploring looks!
You don't die for *your* sins but *mine*! With a bleeding heart
I've murdered seven wives in self-defence. There's something
tragic in the role of Bluebeard. All his wives put together
didn't suffer as much when he strangled them as he did each
time!
But my conscience will be at peace, my body will get stronger
when you no longer dwell in the red silk cushions of my
jewelry box. Now I shall open my opulent pleasure dome to
portraits of The Puritan Maid, Mary Magdalen, The
Respectable Farmer's Wife — and then I'll get over you
sooner. Perhaps in another three months, my angel, your
naked flesh-pot would have started to gnaw my brains like the
sun melting butter pudding. It's time we were granted a
decree!
Ugh, I feel a Heliogabalus rising in me! Moritura me salutat!

Girl, girl why d'you press your knees together — even now when you stand before eternity? *One* tremble, and I'll set you free! *One* feminine wriggle, *one* flicker of lust, of pity, woman! I'd let you lie in a gold frame over my bed! Don't you know it's your respectability that drives me to my debaucheries? Alas, alas, so much inhumanity! One always notices her sort had a good upbringing! It's exactly the same with me! Have you prayed tonight, Desdemona?
My heart breaks. Rot! Even St. Agnes had to die for her virginity, and she wasn't half as naked as you! One last kiss on your blooming body, your girlish, budding breasts, your sweet curved — your cruel knees . . .
It is the cause, it is the cause, my soul! Let me not name it to you, you chaste stars! It is the cause!

The picture falls into the depths. He shuts the lid.

SCENE FOUR

A hayloft.

MELCHIOR *lies on his back in fresh hay.* WENDLA *comes up the ladder.*

WENDLA. *Here's* where you've crept to! They're all looking for you. The hay wagon's gone out again. You've got to help. There's a storm coming.

MELCHIOR. Go away. Go away.

WENDLA. What is it? Why are you hiding your face?

MELCHIOR. Get out! I'll throw you down on the threshing floor!

WENDLA. Now I certainly won't go. (*Kneels beside him.*) Come out in the fields with me, Melchior? It's sticky and gloomy here. It doesn't matter to us if we get soaked!

MELCHIOR. The hay smells so good. The sky outside must be as dark as the grave. All I can see is the bright poppy on your breast — I can hear your heartbeat . . .

WENDLA. Don't kiss me, Melchior! Don't kiss me!

MELCHIOR. Your heart — listen to it beating.

WENDLA. You love each other — when you kiss — no, no!
MELCHIOR. O, believe me, there's no such thing as *love*! It's all
    self, all ego. I don't love you anymore than you love me.
WENDLA. Don't! Don't, Melchior!
MELCHIOR. Wendla!
WENDLA. O, Melchior! Don't, don't.

SCENE FIVE

FRAU GABOR *sits and writes.*

FRAU GABOR. Dear Herr Stiefel,
    After twenty-four hours of thinking and thinking over what
    you have written to me, I take up my pen with a heavy heart.
    I cannot, I give you my solemn word, obtain the cost of a
    passage to America for you. Firstly, I do not have that much
    at my disposal, and secondly, if I had, it would be the greatest
    possible sin to put into your hands the means of carrying out
    a recklessness so fraught with consequence. You would do me
    a grave injustice, Herr Stiefel, if you found in this refusal a
    sign of any lack of love on my part. On the contrary, it would
    be a grave offence to my duty as a motherly friend if I also
    were to lose my head and, influenced by your momentary
    desperation, abandon myself to first impulses. I will gladly,
    should you so wish, write to your parents and try to persuade
    them that throughout this term you have done all that lay in
    your power, and exhausted your strength — so much so that
    any rigorous condemnation of your failure would not only be
    unjust but might very well be detrimental to your physical
    and spiritual health.
    The threat hinted at in your letter — that if your escape were
    not made possible you would take your life — does to be
    frank, Herr Stiefel, somewhat surprise me. Be a misfortune
    never so undeserved, one should not allow oneself to stoop to
    underhand methods. The method by which you seek to make
    me, who have always been kind to you, responsible for any
    ensuing tragedy, smacks somewhat of that which in the eyes
    of ill-disposed persons might well be taken as an attempt at

extortion. I must own that, least of all from you, who otherwise know so well the respect one owes oneself, was the above mentioned to be expected. However, I am convinced that you were still suffering from the effects of first shock and therefore unable to understand the nature of your conduct. And so I confidently trust that these my words will reach you in an already more composed frame of mind. Take things for what they are. In my opinion it is quite wrong to judge a young man by his examination results. We have too many instances before us of bad scholars who became remarkable men, and, contrariwise, of splendid scholars who did not especially prove themselves in later life. Be that as it may, I give you my assurance that, so far as lies within my power, your misfortune shall in no way alter your relations with Melchior. It will always afford me joy to watch my son's intercourse with a young man who, let the world judge him how it may, will always be able to command my fullest sympathy. And therefore, head up, Herr Stiefel. These crises come to us all in one form or another and must be seen through. If we immediately resort to dagger and poison there will very soon be no one left in the world. Let me hear a line from you before long. The very best wishes of your staunch devoted motherly friend Fanny G.

SCENE SIX

The BERGMANNS' *garden in morning sunlight.*

WENDLA. Why did you slip out of the room? To pick violets! Because mother sees me smiling. Why can't you close your lips anymore? I don't know. I really don't know, I don't know the words . . .
The path's like a soft carpet. No stones, no thorns. My feet don't touch the ground . . . O how I slept last night! They were here. I feel as solemn as a nun at communion. These beautiful violets! Hush, mother, I'll wear my sackcloth. O God, if only someone could come and I could throw my arms round his neck and tell!

SCENE SEVEN

Evening, dusk.

The sky is lightly clouded, the path winds between low bushes and reeds. The river is heard a little way off.

MORITZ. The sooner the better. I don't belong here. Let them kick each other to bits. I'll shut the door behind me and walk away into freedom. Why should I let them push me about? I didn't force myself on them. Why should I force myself on them now? I haven't got a contract with God. Look at it from any angle you like, they forced me. I don't blame my parents. Still, they were old enough to know what they were doing. I was a baby when I came in the world — or I'd have had enough sense to come as someone else!

I'd have to be off my head: someone gives me a mad dog, and when he won't take his mad dog back *I* play the gentleman and . . .

I'd have to be off my head!

You're born by pure chance and after mature reconsideration you mustn't . . . ? I could die laughing! At least the weather cares. It looked like rain all day and now it's cleared. The strange stillness everywhere. Nothing harsh or loud. The whole world like a fine cobweb. Everything so calm and still. The landscape is a beautiful lullabye. "Sleep, little prince, go to sleep." Fräulein Hectorina's song. A pity she holds her elbows awkwardly! The last time I danced it was the feast of St. Cicelia. Hectorina only dances with young toffs. Her dress was cut so low at the back and the front. Down to the hips at the back, and in front down to — you mustn't think about it. She couldn't have had a bodice on . . . That might keep me here. More out of curiosity. It must be a strange sensation — like being dragged over maelstroms. I won't tell anyone I've come back half-cocked. I'll behave as if I've done everything. It's shameful to have been a man and not known the most human thing. You come from *Egypt*, dear sir, and you've never seen the pyramids?

I don't want to cry anymore. Or think about my funeral.

Melchior will lay a wreath on my coffin. Reverend Baldbelly
will console my parents. The Head will cite examples from
history. I don't suppose I'll get a tombstone. I'd have liked a
snow-white marble urn on a black syenite column — luckily
I won't miss it. Monuments are for the living not the dead.
It would take at least a year to go through everyone in my
head and say goodbye. I don't want to cry now. I'm glad I can
look back without bitterness. The beautiful evenings with
Melchior! — under the willows, the forester's hut, the old
battleground with the five lime trees, the quiet ruins of the
castle. When the moment comes I'll think with my whole being
of whipped cream. Whipped cream won't stop me. It leaves
behind a pleasant aftertaste, it doesn't end up in your trousers
. . . And then I've always thought people were worse than they
are. I've never met one who didn't try his best. I felt sorry for
them because they had me to deal with.
I go to the altar like an ancient Etruscan youth. His death
rattles bring his brothers prosperity for the year ahead. Drop
by drop I drink the dregs. The secret shudders of crossing over.
I weep with the sadness of my lot. Life gave me the cold
shoulder. From the other side solemn, friendly faces beckon
me: the headless queen, the headless queen — compassion,
waiting for me, with open arms . . . The laws of this world are
for children, I've earned my pass. The balance sinks, the
butterfly rises and flies away. The painted veil no longer blinds
me. Why should I play this mad game with Illusion? The mists
part! Life is a question of taste.

> ILSE, *in torn clothes and with a coloured scarf on her head,*
> *taps his shoulder from behind.*

ILSE. What have you lost?
MORITZ. Ilse?
ILSE. What are you looking for?
MORITZ. Why did you frighten me?
ILSE. What are you looking for? What have you lost?
MORITZ. Why did you frighten me like that?
ILSE. I've just come from town. I'm going home.
MORITZ. I don't know what I've lost.
ILSE. No use looking for it then.

MORITZ. Blast! Blast!

ILSE. I haven't been home for four days.

MORITZ. Creeping about like a cat.

ILSE. I've got my dancing shoes on. Mother's eyes will pop out.
Walk back to our house with me.

MORITZ. Where have you been this time?

ILSE. With the Phallustics!

MORITZ. Phallustics!

ILSE. With Nohl, Karl, Paganini, Schiller, Rank, Dostoevsky —
with anyone I could! O, mother will jump!

MORITZ. Do you sit for them?

ILSE. Karl's painting me as an eremite. I stand on a Corinthian
column. Karl's off his head, believe me. Last time I trod on his
tube of paint. He wiped his brush in my hair. I boxed his ears.
He threw his palette at me. I knock the easel down. He chases
me with his paint stick over the divan, tables, chairs, round
and round the studio. There's a drawing by the fire. Behave or
I'll tear it! He says he'll behave and then ends up kissing me
terribly-terribly, believe me.

MORITZ. Where d'you spend the nights when you're in town?

ILSE. Yesterday at Nohl's — the day before at El Greco's —
Sunday with Bojokewitsch. We had champagne at Paganini's.
Velazquez sold his Plague Sufferer. Adolar drank out of the
ashtray. Schiller sang "The Mother who Murdered her Child"
and Adolar beat hell out of the guitar. I was so drunk they had
to put me to bed. You're still at school, Moritz?

MORITZ. No, no — this is my last term.

ILSE. That's right. O, time passes much better when you're
earning. D'you remember how we played bandits? Wendla
Bergmann and you and me and the others. You all came to
our place in the evenings and drank the goat's milk while it
was still warm. What's Wendla up to? Last time I saw her was
at the flood. What does Melchior Gabor do? Does he still look
so solemn? We used to stand opposite each other in music.

MORITZ. He's a philosopher.

ILSE. Wendla was at our place a while back and brought mother
some stewed fruit. I was sitting for Isidor Landauer then. He
wants me for the Virgin Mary, the mother of God with the
baby Jesus. He's an idiot and disgusting. Ugh, never settles.

Have you got a hangover?

MORITZ. From last night. We knocked it back like
hippopotamuses. I staggered home at five.

ILSE. You've only got to look at you! Were there any girls?

MORITZ. Arabella. We drank beer out of her slipper. She's
Spanish, you know. The landlord left us alone with her the
whole night.

ILSE. You've only got to look at you, Moritz! I don't know what
a hangover is! Last carnival I didn't go to bed or get out of my
clothes for three days and nights! From Fancy Dress Balls to
the cafés, lunch on the lake, cellar revues in the evenings,
nights back to the Fancy Dress Balls. Lena was with me and
that fat Viola. Heinrich found me on the third night.

MORITZ. Was he looking for you?

ILSE. He tripped over my arm. I was lying unconscious on the
street in the snow. Afterwards I went back to his place. I
couldn't get away for two weeks — that was a terrible time!
Every morning I had to pose in his Persian dressing gown, and
every evening walk round his rooms in a black page-boy tunic.
White lace, cuffs, collar and knees. He photographed me in a
different way every day — once as Ariadne on the arm of the
sofa, once as Leda, once as Ganymede, and once on all fours
as a female Nobobycanesor. He was always squirming on
about murder, shooting, suicide, drugs and fumes. He brought
a pistol in bed every morning, loaded it with shot, and pushed
it into my breast: one twitch and I press. O, he would have
pressed, Moritz, he would have pressed. Then he put the thing
in his mouth like a pea-shooter. It's supposed to be good for
the self-preservation instinct. Ugh — the bullet would have
gone through my spine!

MORITZ. Is Heinrich still alive?

ILSE. How should I know? There was a big mirror in the ceiling
over the bed. The little room looked as tall as a tower, as
bright as an opera house. You saw yourself hanging down alive
from the sky. I had terrible dreams. God, o God, if only the
day would come. Good night, Ilse. When you're asleep you're
so beautiful I could murder you.

MORITZ. Is this Heinrich still alive?

ILSE. No, please God. One day he was fetching absinthe and I

threw my coat on and slipped out in the street. The carnival
was over. The police picked me up. What was I doing in men's
clothes? They took me to the station. Then Nohl, Karl,
Paganini, Schiller and El Greco, all the Phallustics, came and
stood bail for me. They carried me home in a posh cab. Since
then I've stuck to the crowd. Karl's an ape, Nohl's a pig,
Berlioz's goat, Dostoevsky's a hyena, El Greco's a bear —
but I love them, all of them together, and I wouldn't trust
anyone else even if the world was full of saints and millionaires.

MORITZ. I must go home, Ilse.

ILSE. Come back to my place.

MORITZ. Why? Why . . . ?

ILSE. To drink warm goat's milk. I'll curl your hair and hang a
bell round your neck. Or there's a rocking-horse you can play
on.

MORITZ. I must go home. I've still got the Sassanids, the sermon
on the mount, and the Parallelepipedon on my conscience.
Good night, Ilse.

ILSE. Sleep tight! D'you still play in the wigwam where Melchior
Gabor buried my tomahawk? Ugh! Before you're ready I'll be
in the dustbin. (*She hurries away.*)

MORITZ (*alone*). One word! That's all it needed! (*Calls.*) Ilse!
Ilse! Thank God she can't hear.
I'm not in the mood. You have to be clear-headed and relaxed
for that. Pity, pity — a wasted chance.
I'll say I had huge crystal mirrors over my beds and reared an
untamed colt and let it prance round me on carpets in long
black silk stockings and shiny black boots and long black kid
gloves and black velvet round its throat and in an insane
frenzy I took the pillow and smothered it — I will smile when
they talk of lust — I will — scream! — Scream! To be you, Ilse!
Phallic! Unselfconscious! That's what takes my strength
away! That happy child, that child of nature — that little
whore on my path of misery!
(*In the bushes on the bank.*) I've come here again without
knowing it . . . the grass bank. The rods of the bulrushes look
taller since yesterday. The view through the willows is the
same. The river passes as slowly as melted lead. I mustn't
forget . . . (*He takes* FRAU GABOR's *letter from his pocket,*

and burns it.) How the sparks float . . . here and there, round and round — souls! Shooting stars!
Before I made the flame I could see the rushes and a line on the horizon. Now it's dark. I shan't go home now.

Act Three

SCENE ONE

Staff room.

Portraits of Pestalozzi and J.J. Rousseau. Gas-lamps burn over a green table. At the table sit PROFESSORS APELARD, THICKSTICK, GUTGRINDER, BONEBREAKER, TONGUE-TWISTER *and* FLYSWATTER. HEADMASTER SUNSTROKE *sits at the head of the table on a raised chair. The School Porter* FASTCRAWLER *huddles by the door.*

SUNSTROKE. Would any gentleman care to add any further remarks? Gentlemen! We cannot for the gravest of reasons abstain from asking the Minister of State for Cultural Affairs for the expulsion of our guilt-laden student. We cannot abstain so as to atone for the disaster that has already befallen us, and no less we cannot so as to secure our Institution against similar blows. We cannot abstain so as to chastise our guilt-laden student for the demoralising influence he has borne over his fellow students, and no less we cannot so as to prevent the further bearing of that demoralising influence. We cannot abstain — and here, gentlemen, might lie our most compelling reason, whereby whatsoever objections that are raised may be utterly crushed — so as to protect our Institution from the devastation of a suicide epidemic which has already come to pass in other Institutions and which has rendered, until now, our scholarly task of uniting our scholars by means of the fruits of scholarly instruction to the fruition of the life of scholarship, ridiculous. Would any gentlemen care to add any further remarks?

THICKSTICK. I can no longer close my mind to the conviction that the time has come when the opening of a window should be permitted somewhere.

TONGUETWISTER. The at-atmosphere here is dom-dominated

by a resemblance to the subterranean cat-catacombs of a medieval a-a-a-ssize!

SUNSTROKE. Fastcrawler!

FASTCRAWLER. Present, sir!

SUNSTROKE. Open a window. Thanks to God we have sufficient atmosphere outside. Would any gentlemen care to add any further remarks?

FLYSWATTER. Should any of my colleagues wish to permit the opening of a window I for my part raise no objection. I would merely request that the window permitted to be open is not immediately in the back of my neck!

SUNSTROKE. Fastcrawler!

FASTCRAWLER. Present, sir!

SUNSTROKE. Open the other window. Would any gentlemen care to add any further remarks?

GUTGRINDER. Without in any way wishing to complicate the issue I would ask you to recall that since the long holidays the other window has been bricked up.

SUNSTROKE. Fastcrawler!

FASTCRAWLER. Present, sir!

SUNSTROKE. Let the other window be shut. I see myself forced, gentlemen, to put the matter to a vote. I call upon those colleagues who are in favour of permitting the opening of the only window that now comes into question, to rise from their seats. (*He counts.*) One, two, three. Fastcrawler!

FASTCRAWLER. Present, sir!

SUNSTROKE. Leave the other window shut as well. For my part I hold to my conviction that the atmosphere here leaves nothing to be desired. Would any gentlemen care to add any further remarks? Gentlemen! Let us suppose that we were to abstain from requesting the Minister of State for Cultural Affaires for the expulsion of our guilt-laden student — then *we* would be held responsible for the disaster that has befallen us. Of the various schools plagued by suicide epidemics the Minister has already shut down those in which the devastion has claimed a sacrifice of twenty-five percent. It is our duty as guardians and defenders of our Institution to defend it against so shattering a blow. It deeply pains us, my dear colleagues, that we find ourselves in no position to take into account the mitigating features presented by our guilt-laden student. An indulgent approach that left us blameless in our handling of our guilt-laden student would *not* leave us blameless in our handling of the at present highly probable threat to the existence of our Institution. We see ourselves forced to judge the guilty so as not to be judged guilty ourselves! Fastcrawler!

FASTCRAWLER. Present, sir!

SUNSTROKE. Fetch him up.

FASTCRAWLER *goes.*

TONGUETWISTER. If the dom-dominating at-at-atmosphere officially leaves nothing to be desired might I then pro-propose the motion that the other window also be bricked u-u-u-u-u-u-u-u-u-u-u-up?

FLYSWATTER. Should it appear to our respected colleague that our room is not sufficiently ventilated, might I propose the motion that he has a ventilator bored in the top of his head?

TONGUETWISTER. I do-do-don't have to put up with that! I do-do-don't have to put up with rudeness! I'm in possession of all my f-f-f-f-five senses!

SUNSTROKE. I must call upon our colleagues Flyswatter and Tonguetwister for a show of decorum. Our guilt laden student stands at the door.

FASTCRAWLER *opens the door, and* MELCHIOR *steps in front of the meeting. He is pale but composed.*

SUNSTROKE. Step closer to the table. After the respectable landlord Herr Stiefel had been informed of his late son's unseemly misconduct, that bewildered father searched, in the hope that he might come across the cause of this disgusting crime, in the remaining effects of his son Moritz and found, in an at the moment irrelevant place, a handwritten document which, without in any way making this disgusting crime at all comprehensible, does afford us an, alas, all too clear insight into the criminal's state of moral chaos. I refer to a handwritten document in dialogue-form entitled *"On Copulation"*, replete with life-size illustrations, and crammed with obscenities so shameless that they might well satisfy the utmost demands for depravity that a degenerate lecher could make on obscene literature.

MELCHIOR. I have . . .

SUNSTROKE. You have to be silent. After Herr Stiefel had put the document in question into our <u>hands</u> and we had given the bewildered father our solemn word to at all costs ascertain its author, the handwriting was compared with the handwriting of every fellow student of the deceased malpractiser and matched, according to the unanimous verdict of the whole faculty and in complete agreement with the expert opinion of our honoured colleague the Professor of Calligraphy, yours.

MELCHIOR. I have . . .

SUNSTROKE. You have to be silent. Notwithstanding the over-whelming evidence of this identification, acceded to by such unimpeachable authorities, we believe ourselves able to refrain from precipitate action for the moment, and to instead impartially interrogate you about the crime against morality of which you stand accused and which served as an incitement to self-destruction.

MELCHIOR. I have . . .

SUNSTROKE. You have to answer the precisely phrased questions, which I shall put to you one after the other, with a simple and respectful yes or no. Fastcrawler!

FASTCRAWLER. Present, sir!

SUNSTROKE. The file. I request our secretary, Herr Flyswatter, to take down the protocol from now on word for word as exactly as possible. (To MELCHIOR.) Do you know this document?

MELCHIOR. Yes.

SUNSTROKE. Do you know what this document contains?

MELCHIOR. Yes.

SUNSTROKE. Is the handwriting in this document yours?

MELCHIOR. Yes.

SUNSTROKE. Does this obscene document owe its manufacture to you?

MELCHIOR. Yes. Sir, I ask you to show me one obscenity in it.

SUNSTROKE. You have to answer the precisely phrased questions, which I shall put to you, with a simple and respectful yes or no.

MELCHIOR. I've written no more and no less than everyone of
   you knows to be a fact.
SUNSTROKE. This insolent puppy!
MELCHIOR. I ask you to show me one offence against morality
   in that paper!
SUNSTROKE. Do you imagine that I will stand here and let
   myself become the butt of your jests? Fastcrawler!
MELCHIOR. I have . . .
SUNSTROKE. You have as little respect for the dignity of your
   assembled masters as you have for mankind's sense of shame
   when confronted with the moral order of the universe.
   Fastcrawler!
FASTCRAWLER. Present, sir!
SUNSTROKE. This is the definitive text on how to learn
   Esperanto in three easy months without a master!
MELCHIOR. I have . . .
SUNSTROKE. I call upon our secretary to close the protocol.
MELCHIOR. I have . . .
SUNSTROKE. You have to be silent. Fastcrawler!
FASTCRAWLER. Present, sir!
SUNSTROKE. Put him down.

SCENE TWO

Churchyard in pouring rain.

REVEREND BALDBELLY *stands in front of the open grave
with an umbrella in his hand. On his right* HERR STIEFEL, *his
friend* GOAT *and* UNCLE PROBST. *On the left* HEADMASTER
SUNSTROKE *and* PROFESSOR BONEBREAKER. STUDENTS
make up the rest of a circle. Some distance off MARTHA *and*
ILSE *stand by a half-fallen grave stone.*

BALDBELLY. Whosoever spurns the grace with which the
   Eternal Father blesses all who are born in sin, he shall die the
   death of the spirit. And whosoever in flesh and pride denies
   the worship owed to God and lives and serves evil, he shall die
   the death of the body. But whosoever sacrilegiously casts

aside the cross with which the Almighty inflicts this life of sin, verily, verily I say unto you, he shall die the eternal death. (*He throws a shovel of earth into the grave*.) But we who go forth on the path of thorns, let us praise the Lord, the All Merciful, and thank him for his unsearchable gift of predestination. For as surely as this died the three-fold death, as surely will Lord God lead the righteous to salvation and eternal life. Amen.

HERR STIEFEL (*with tear-choked voice as he throws a shovel of earth into the grave*). That boy wasn't mine. That boy wasn't mine. I had my doubts about that boy since he was a tot.

SUNSTROKE. (*throws a shovel of earth into the grave*). While suicide is the greatest conceivable offence against the moral order of the universe, it is at the same time the greatest conceivable proof *of* the moral order of the universe, in that the suicide spares the moral order of the universe the necessity of pronouncing its verdict and so confirms its existence.

BONEBREAKER (*throws a shovel of earth into the grave*). Dilatory — dissipated — debauched — dissolute — and dirty!

UNCLE PROBST (*throws a shovel of earth into the grave*). I would not have believed my own mother if she'd told me a child would treat its parents so basely.

FRIEND GOAT (*throws a shovel of earth into the grave*). To do that to a father who for twenty years cherished no other thought from morning till night than the welfare of his son!

BALDBELLY (*shaking HERR STIEFEL'S hand*). We know that they who love God make all things serve the best. Corinthians I, 14:12. Think of the comfortless mother and try to replace her loss by redoubled love.

SUNSTROKE. (*shaking HERR STIEFEL's hand*). And after all it's clear that we might well not have been able to promote him anyway.

BONEBREAKER (*shaking HERR STIEFEL's hand*). And if we had promoted him he'd certainly have been left standing next spring.

UNCLE PROBST (*shaking HERR STIEFEL's hand*). It's your duty to think of yourself before everything else now. You are head of a family . . .

FRIEND GOAT (*shaking HERR STIEFEL's hand*). Take my arm.

Cats-and-dogs weather, enough to wring the bowels. If we
don't all immediately perform the vanishing trick with a glass
of hot punch we'll catch a heart condition!

HERR STIEFEL (*blowing his nose*). That boy wasn't mine. That
boy wasn't mine.

> HERR STIEFEL *is lead away by* PASTOR BALDBELLY,
> HEADMASTER SUNSTROKE, PROFESSOR BONE-
> BREAKER, UNCLE PROBST *and* FRIEND GOAT.
> *The rain lessens.*

HÄNSCHEN (*throws a shovel of earth into the grave*). Rest in
peace, poor sod. Give my regards to my dead brides — and
put in a word for me to God, you poor fool. You're so
innocent they'll have to put something on your grave to scare
the birds off.

GEORG. Did they find the pistol?

ROBERT. There's no point in looking for a pistol.

ERNST. Did you see him, Robert?

ROBERT. Rotten, blasted swizz! Who saw him? Anyone?

OTTO. That's the mystery! They threw a cloth over him.

GEORG. Did his tongue hang out?

ROBERT. The eyes! That's why they threw the cloth over him.

OTTO. Horrible!

HÄNSCHEN. Are you sure he hanged himself?

ERNST. They say he's got no head now.

OTTO. Rubbish! All talk!

ROBERT. I had the rope in my hand. They always cover up a
hanged man.

GEORG. He couldn't have chosen a more small-minded way of
going off.

HÄNSCHEN. What the hell, hanging's supposed to be fun!

OTTO. The fact is, he still owes me five marks. We had a bet. He
swore he'd be promoted.

HÄNSCHEN. It's your fault he's down there. You said he was
bragging.

OTTO. Rot! I have to slave through the nights too. If he'd
learned his Greek history he wouldn't have had to hang
himself.

ERNST. Have you done your essay, Otto?

OTTO. Only the start.

ERNST. I don't know what we're supposed to write about.

GEORG. Weren't you there when Apelard gave it out?

HANSCHEN. I'll stick together some bits of Democrites.

ERNST. I'll get something out of the reference library.

OTTO. Have you done tomorrow's Virgil?

The STUDENTS *go.* MARTHA *and* ILSE *come to the grave.*

ILSE. Quick, quick! The gravediggers are coming over there.

MARTHA. Shouldn't we wait?

ILSE. What for? We'll bring fresh ones. Always fresh, fresh! They grow everywhere!

MARTHA. That's right, Ilse. (*She throws an ivy wreath into the grave.* ILSE *opens her apron and lets a stream of fresh anemones fall onto the coffin.*) I'll dig up our roses. I get beaten anyway. They'll grow so well here.

ILSE. I'll water them every time I go by. I'll bring forget-me-nots from the brook and irises from home.

MARTHA. It'll become a marvel!

ILSE. I'd already crossed the bridge when I heard the bang.

MARTHA. Poor thing.

ILSE. And I know why, Martha.

MARTHA. Did he tell you something?

ILSE. He was on parallelepipedon! Don't tell.

MARTHA. Cross my heart.

ILSE. Here's the pistol.

MARTHA. That's why they couldn't find it.

ILSE. I took it straight out of his hand when I went by.

MARTHA. Let's have it, Ilse! Let's have it, please!

ILSE. No, it's my keepsake.

MARTHA. Ilse, is it true he's down there with no head?

ILSE. He must have loaded it with water. His blood was spattered round and round on the bulrushes. His brains were hanging all over the willows.

SCENE THREE

HERR *and* FRAU GABOR.

FRAU GABOR. . . . They needed a scapegoat. The accusations were getting louder and they couldn't wait for them to die down. And because Melchior had the misfortune to cross those pedants just at this moment, shall I, his mother, help the hangmen to finish their work? God keep me from such a thing!

HERR GABOR. For fourteen years I've silently observed your imaginative methods of rearing children. They contradicted my own convistions. I have always lived by the conviction that a child isn't a toy. A child has a right to our solemn seriousness. But I told myself, if spirit and grace can replace serious principles, then they might be preferable to serious principles. I'm not blaming you, Fanny. But don't stand in my way when I try to make amends for the wrong you and I have done the boy.

FRAU GABOR. I'll stand in your way as long as there's a drop of human blood in me! My child would be lost in a reformatory. A natural criminal might be made better in such an institution. I don't know. But a decent nature will be made criminal just as a plant dies when it's taken from the light. I'm not aware of any wrong. I thank God now, as I always have, for showing me how to make my child decent and honest. What has he done that's so terrible? It would never enter my head to make excuses for him — but it's not his fault he's been hounded out of school! And if it had been his fault he's certainly paid for it! You may understand these things better than I do. Theoretically you may be perfectly right. But I will not allow my son to be brutally hounded to his death!

HERR GABOR. That doesn't depend on us, Fanny, that's the risk that went with our happiness. He who's too weak falls by the wayside. And in the end it's not the worst if the inevitable comes on time. May heaven spare us that! Our duty now is to strengthen the waverer, so long as reason shows us how. It's not his fault they hounded him out of school. If they hadn't hounded him out that wouldn't be his fault either! You're too

easy going. You see minor peccadillos when we are faced with
fundamental defects of character. Women aren't called on to
judge these things. Whoever can write what Melchior wrote
must be contaminated in his innermost core. The marrow is
effected. Even a nature only half-sound couldn't bring itself to
that! None of us are saints, we all stray from the way. But his
document is grounded in Principle. It doesn't suggest one
accidental false step, it documents with terrifying clarity an
openly cherished talent, a natural propensity, for the Immoral
for the sake of the Immoral. It shows that rare spiritual
corruption we lawyers call "moral insanity". Whether anything
can be done about his condition, it's not for me to say. If we
wish to preserve one glimmer of hope, and above all keep our
consciences unsullied as the parents of the culprit, then we must
act with resolution and determination. Don't let's quarrel
anymore, Fanny! I know how hard this is for you. You
worship him because he matches your own generous nature. so
well. Rise above yourself! For once act unselfishly in your
relations with your son.

FRAU GABOR. O God — how can one fight against it! Only a
man can talk like that. Only a man can be so blinded by the
dead letter he can't see what's staring him in the face! I've
handled Melchior responsibly and carefully from the beginning.
Are we to blame for this coincidence? Tomorrow a tile could
fall on your head and your friend comes — your father, and
instead of tending your wounds he treads on you! I will not let
my child be taken out and murdered in front of my eyes.
That's what his mother's for! — I cannot understand it. It's
beyond belief. What in the world has he written? Isn't it the
clearest proof of his harmlessness, his silliness, his child-like
innocence, that he *can* write something like that? You don't
need to know much about people — you must be an utterly
soulless bureaucrat or totally shrivelled up, to see moral
corruption in that! Say what you like. When you put Melchior
in a reformatory, I shall divorce you! And then I shall see if
somewhere in the world I can't find help to save my son from
destruction.

HERR GABOR. You will have to give in — if not today then
tomorrow. It's not easy for any of us to discount our

misfortunes. I shall stand by you when your courage fails, I
shall begrudge no effort or sacrifice to lighten your burden. I
see the future so grey, so overcast — it only needs you to be
lost to me now.

FRAU GABOR. I'll never see him again. I'll never see him again.
He can't bear vulgarity. He can't live with filth. He'll lose all
restraints — that terrible example is before his eyes! And if I
saw him again — O God, God, that heart full of spring — that
bright laughter — all, all — his young determination to fight
for everything that's good and just — as bright and fresh as the
morning sky — that boy I cherished as my highest good! Take
me if his crime cries out for retribution! Take me! Do what
you want with me! Let me bear the guilt! But keep your
terrible hand away from my child.

HERR GABOR. He has offended!

FRAU GABOR. *He has not offended!*

HERR GABOR. *He has* offended! I would have given anything
to spare your boundless love for him. This morning a woman
came to me, like a ghost, hardly able to speak, with *this* letter
in her hand — a letter to her fifteen year-old daughter. Out of
silly curiosity she'd opened it — her daughter was not at home.
In the letter Melchior explains to the fifteen year-old child
that his conduct gives him no peace, he has wronged her
etcetera etcetera. She is not to worry, even if she suspects
consequences. He is already taking steps to find help, his
expulsion makes that easier. The earlier wrong may yet lead
to their happiness — and more of the same meaningless chatter.

FRAU GABOR. I don't believe it!

HERR GABOR. The letter is forged. It's an attack. Someone
trying to use an expulsion that's already known to the whole
town. I haven't yet spoken to the boy — but kindly look at
the hand. Look at the writing.

FRAU GABOR. An unheard of, shameless infamy!

HERR GABOR. I fear so!

FRAU GABOR. No, no — never.

HERR GABOR. Then all the better for us. The woman stood
wringing her hands and asking me what she should do. I told
her not to let her fifteen-year-old daughter climb about in
haylofts. As luck would have it she left the letter with me. If

we send Melchior away to another school, where he wouldn't even be under parental supervision, we'll have another incident within three weeks — another expulsion — his spring-like heart is already getting used to it. Tell me, Fanny, where shall I put the boy?

FRAU GABOR. In the reformatory.

HERR GABOR. The . . . ?

FRAU GABOR. Reformatory.

HERR GABOR. Above all, he'll find there what he was unjustly denied at home: iron discipline, principles and a moral force under which he must at all times subordinate himself. By the way, the reformatory isn't the chamber of horrors you imagine. It lays its main emphasis on developing Christian thinking and sensibility. The boy will finally learn there to put the good before the interesting, and to act not according to his nature but according to the rules. Half an hour ago I had a telegramme from my brother, which confirms the deposition of that woman. Melchior has confided in him and asked for money for their flight to England . . .

FRAU GABOR. *(covers her face)*. God have mercy on us!

SCENE FOUR

Reformatory. A corridor.

DIETER, REINHOLD, RUPERT, HELMUT, GASTON *and* MELCHIOR.

DIETER. Here's a coin.

REINHOLD. What for?

DIETER. Drop it on the floor. Spread yourselves out. The one who hits it, keeps it.

RUPERT. Coming in, Melchior.

MELCHIOR. No thanks.

HELMUT. Git!

GASTON. He can't anymore. He's here for the rest cure.

MELCHIOR *(to himself)*. It's not clever to stay out. They're all watching me. I'll join in — or I've had it. Being shut up makes them suicidal. If you break your neck it's all right! If you get

out it's all right! You can only win! Rupert looks friendly,
he'll show me round. I'll teach him about the Bible — how Lot
got drunk and slept with his daughters and offered them to
other men, how David was a Peeping Tom who slept with a
soldier's wife and warmed his bed with a beautiful virgin called
Abishay the Shunnamite. He's got the unluckiest face in my
squad.

RUPERT. Coming!

HELMUT. I'm coming too.

GASTON. Day after tomorrow if you're lucky!

HELMUT. Hold on! Now! Jesus — Jesus.

ALL. Altogether now! — Ten out of ten!

RUPERT. (taking the coin). Ta, very much.

HELMUT. That's mine, pig!

RUPERT. Animal!

HELMUT. They'll top you!

RUPERT (hits him in the face). For that? (Turns and runs away.)

HELMUT (chasing him). I'll kick your head off!

THE OTHERS (chasing them). Get him, after him! Get him! Get
him! Get him!

MELCHIOR (alone, turns to the window). That's where the
lightning conductor goes down. You'd have to wrap a
handkerchief round . . . When I think of her the blood goes to
my head, and Moritz is like a chain round my feet. I'll try the
newspapers. Become a hack. They pay by the hundred lines.
News, gossip, articles — ethics — psychology. You can't starve
now! Soup kitchens, hostels. — This building is sixty feet high
and the plaster's falling off . . . She hates me — I took her
freedom away. Whatever I do now, it's still rape. But later on
perhaps she'll . . . I must hope. The new moon in eight days. I'll
grease the hinges. Find out who has the key. On Sunday night
I'll have a fit in the chapel. I hope to God no one else is ill! I'll
slip over the sill — swing — grab — but you must wrap a handkerchief round . . . Here comes the Grand Inquisitor. (Goes off
left).

DR. PROCRUSTES comes on right with a LOCKSMITH.

PROCRUSTES. Undoubtedly the windows are on the fourth floor,
and I've planted stinging nettles underneath. But what are

stinging nettles to degenerates? Last winter one of them
climbed out of the skylight. We had all the fuss of fetching,
carrying, interning . . .

LOCKSMITH. Would you like the grating in wrought iron?

PROCRUSTES. Wrought iron — and since you can't build it into
the wall, rivet it.

SCENE FIVE

A bedroom.

FRAU BERGMANN, INA MÜLLER *and* DR. LEMONADE.
WENDLA *in bed.*

DR. LEMONADE. How old are you actually?

WENDLA. Fourteen and a half.

DR. LEMONADE. I've prescribed purgative pills for fifteen years
and in a large number of cases witnessed the most dazzling
success. I place them above codliver oil and iron tonic. Start
with three or four pills a day and increase the dosage just as
fast as you can tolerate them. I advised Fräulein Elfriede
Baroness von Witzleben to increase the dose by one pill every
third day. The baroness misunderstood me and increased the
dose by three pills every day. After barely three weeks the
baroness could already proceed with her lady mother to an
exclusive spa in the mountains. I excuse you from all fatiguing
walks and special diets. But you must promise me, dear child,
to keep moving and not be too shy to ask for food as soon as
the desire for it returns. Then this wind round the heart will
go away, and the headaches, the shivering, the dizzyness — and
our terrible indigestion. Only eight days after starting the cure
Fräulein Elfriede Baroness von Witzleben could already eat a
whole roast chicken with new boiled potatoes for breakfast.

FRAU BERGMANN. May I offer you a glass of wine, Doctor?

DR. LEMONADE. Thank you kindly, dear Frau Bergmann. My
patients await me. Don't take it too much to heart. In a few
weeks our charming little patient will once more be as fresh
and lively as a sprite. Rest assured. Good day, Frau Bergmann.
Good day, dear child. Good day, ladies. Good day.

FRAU BERGMANN *goes to show him out.*

INA *(at the window).* The leaves on your plane-trees are
changing colour. Can you see it from the bed? They come and
go, a short glory, hardly worth being happy about. I must go
too. Herr Müller's meeting me at the post office, and before
that I have to go to the dressmaker. Mucki's getting his first
trousers, and Karl's going to get a new jersey suit for the
winter.

WENDLA. Sometimes I'm so happy — there's so much joy and
the sunshine is so bright. I want to go out, and walk over the
fields when it's dusk, and look for primroses and sit and dream
by the river. And then this *toothache* starts, and I think that
tomorrow is the day I shall die. I feel hot and cold, everything
goes dark, and the monster flutters in . . . Whenever I wake up
mother's crying. O that hurts so much . . . I can't tell you, Ina.

INA. Shall I lift your pillow?

FRAU BERGMANN *comes back.*

FRAU BERGMANN. He thinks the vomiting will stop and then
it will be safe for you to get up. I think you should get up
soon, too, Wendla.

INA. Perhaps next time I come to see you you'll be jumping
round the house again. Bless you, mother. I really must go to
the dressmaker. God bless you, Wendla, dear. *(Kisses her.)*
Soon, soon better!

WENDLA. Thank you, Ina. Bring me some primroses next time
you come. Goodbye. Say hello to the boys for me.

INA *goes.*

WENDLA. What did he say outside, mother?

FRAU BERGMANN. Nothing. He said Fräulein von Witzleben
also tended to faint. Evidently it almost always happens with
anemia.

WENDLA. Did he say I have anemia, mother?

FRAU BERGMANN. When your appetite returns you're to drink
milk and eat fresh vegetables.

WENDLA. O mother, mother, I don't think I have anemia.

FRAU BERGMANN. You have anemia child. Be quiet, Wendla,

be quiet. You have anemia.

WENDLA. No, mother, no! I know it! I can feel it! I haven't got anemia. I've got dropsy.

FRAU BERGMANN. You have anemia. He said you have anemia. Be quiet, Wendla. It will get better.

WENDLA. It won't get better. I have dropsy. I'm going to die, mother. O mother, I'm going to die.

FRAU BERGMANN. You won't have to die, Wendla. You won't have to die . . . Merciful heaven, you won't have to die.

WENDLA. Then why d'you cry so much?

FRAU BERGMANN. You won't have to die, child! You haven't got dropsy. You have a baby, Wendla! You have a baby! O, why have you done this to me?

WENDLA. I haven't done anything to you . . .

FRAU BERGMANN. O don't keep lying, Wendla! I know everything. I couldn't say it before. Wendla, Wendla . . .

WENDLA. But it's just not possible, mother. I'm not even married.

FRAU BERGMANN. God in heaven — that's just it, you're not married! That's what's so terrible! Wendla, Wendla, Wendla, what have you done?

WENDLA. O God, I don't know anymore. We were lying in the hay — I've never loved anyone in the world except you, you, mother!

FRAU BERGMANN. My precious!

WENDLA. O mother, why didn't you tell me everything?

FRAU BERGMANN. Child, child, don't let's make each other more unhappy. Keep calm. Don't give up hope, my dear! Tell that to a fourteen year-old girl? No, I'd sooner have believed the sun could go out! I did nothing to you my dear mother hadn't done to me! O let us put our trust in the dear lord, Wendla. Let us hope in his mercy, and do our part. Look, so far nothing's happened. And if only we don't become timid now — God's love will not abandon us. *Be brave, be brave, Wendla* . . . Once before I sat with my hands in my lap and stared out of the window, and in the end everything turned out well — and now suddenly the world falls to pieces and my heart breaks . . . why are you shaking?

WENDLA. Someone knocked.

FRAU BERGMANN. I didn't hear anything, my precious. *(Goes*

to the door and opens it.)
WENDLA. O I heard it so clearly. Who's outside?
FRAU BERGMANN. No one. Mr. Schmidt's mother from
    Garden Street. You're just on time, Mrs. Schmidt.

SCENE SIX

MEN *and* WOMEN *working in a hillside vineyard.*

*The sun sets behind the mountains. The clear-toned notes of
bells come up from the valley.* HÄNSCHEN RILOW *and* ERNST
RÖBEL *loll in the dry grass at the top of the vineyard, under
over-hanging rocks.*

ERNST. I've worked too hard.
HÄNSCHEN. We mustn't be sad. Time passes so quickly.
ERNST. The grapes hang there. You can't even reach out for
    them. And tomorrow they're crushed.
HÄNSCHEN. Being tired is as bad as being hungry.
ERNST. O no more.
HÄNSCHEN. That big one.
ERNST. I can't stretch.
HÄNSCHEN. I could bend the branch till it swings between our
    mouths. We needn't move. Just bite the grapes and let the
    branch swing back.
ERNST. You only have to make up your mind — and all your
    old energy gushes up.
HÄNSCHEN. And the flaming sky — the evening bells — I don't
    hope for much more out of life.
ERNST. Sometimes I already see myself as a dignified parson —
    a cheerful little housewife, big library, all sorts of honours and
    decorations. Six days shalt thou labour and on the seventh
    open your mouth. When you're out walking school-children
    greet you politely, and when you get home the coffee's
    steaming, there's home-made cake on the table, and the girls
    are bringing in the apples through the garden door. Can
    anything be better?
HÄNSCHEN. Half-shut eyelashes, half-open mouths, and
    Turkish pillows. I don't believe in the Sentimental. You know,

the old people wear dignified faces to hide their stupidity.
Among themselves they call each other fools just as we do. I
know it. When I'm a millionaire I'll erect a great monument to
God. Think of the future as bread and milk and sugar. Some
people drop it and howl, others stir it till they sweat. Why not
just cream off the top? Or don't you think you can?

ERNST. Let's cream off the top.

HÄNSCHEN. And throw the rest to the chickens. I've already
slipped my head out of so many nooses.

ERNST. Let's cream off the top. Why are you laughing?

HÄNSCHEN. You're off again!

ERNST. Someone's got to start!

HÄNSCHEN. In thirty years when we look back to this evening,
I suppose it could seem incredibly beautiful.

ERNST. And now it just happens!

HÄNSCHEN. Why not?

ERNST. If I was on my own — I might even cry.

HÄNSCHEN. We mustn't be sad. *(Kisses his mouth.)*

ERNST *(kissing him)*. When I left home I only meant to speak to
you and then go back.

HÄNSCHEN. I was waiting for you. Virtue looks good but it only
suits imposing figures.

ERNST. It's several sizes too big for us. I'd have been on edge if
I hadn't met you. I love you, Hänschen, I've never loved
anyone like this —

HÄNSCHEN. We musn't be sad! Perhaps when we look back in
thirty years we'll jeer — but now everything is beautiful.
Glowing mountains, grapes hanging down in our mouths, the
evening wind stroking the rocks like a little kitten playing . . .

SCENE SEVEN

Bright November night.

*Dry leaves rustle on bushes and trees. Torn clouds chase each
other over the moon.* MELCHIOR *climbs over the churchyard
wall.*

MELCHIOR *(jumping down inside)*. That pack won't follow me

here. While they search the brothels, I'll get my breath and
sort myself out . . . Jacket in shreds, pockets empty. I couldn't
defend myself against a child. I'll keep moving through the
woods during the day . . . I knocked a cross down — the frost's
killed all the flowers anyway. Everything's bare! The kingdom
of death!
This is worse than climbing out of the skylight! Like falling
and falling and falling into nothing! I wasn't prepared for this!
I should have stayed where I was!
Why her and not me? Why not the guilty? Providence or a
riddle? I'd break stones, starve — how can I even walk upright?
One crime leads to another: I'll sink in a swamp. I haven't got
the strength to finish it . . . It was not wrong! It was not
wrong! It was not wrong!
No one's ever walked over graves and been so full of envy. No
— I wouldn't have the courage! O, if I could go mad — tonight!
The new ones are over there. The wind whistles on each grave-
stone in a different key — listen, the voices of pain! The
wreaths are rotting on the marble crosses. They fall to pieces
and jog up and down on their long strings. There's a forest of
scarecrows over the graves. Taller than houses. Even the devil
would run away. The gold letters flash so coldly. That's a
willow tree groaning. Its branches are like a giant's fingers
feeling over the epitaphs. A stone angel. A tablet.
That cloud's thrown its shadow on everything. How it races
and howls! Like an army rushing up to the east! And no stars.
There's evergreen round this one. Evergreen? A girl.

> Here rests in God
> Wendla Bergmann
> Born 5 May 1878
> Died of anemia
> 27 October 1892
> Blessed are the pure in heart

And I murdered her. I am her murderer. Now there's nothing.
I musn't cry here. I must go away. I must go.

MORITZ STIEFEL, *with his head under his arm, comes
stamping across the graves.*

MORITZ. One moment, Melchior! This chance won't come again

so soon. You can't know how much depends on time and
place . . .

MELCHIOR. Where have you come form?

MORITZ. Over there by the wall. You knocked my cross down.
I lie by the wall. Give me your hand, Melchior.

MELCHIOR. You are *not* Moritz Stiefel!

MORITZ. Give me your hand. I know you'll be grateful. It will
never be so easy for you again. This is a very lucky meeting. I
came up especially . . .

MELCHIOR. Don't you sleep?

MORITZ. Not what you call sleep. We sit on church towers, on
the roofs of houses — wherever we like . . .

MELCHIOR. At peace?

MORITZ. For pleasure. We ride on the wooden horses at fairs,
and float round empty churches. We fly over great assemblies
of people, over scenes of disaster, gardens, festivals. We crouch
in the corners of people's houses, and wait by their beds. Give
me your hand. The dead are alone, we don't go with each
other, but we see and hear everything that happens in the
world. We know that it's all vanity, the things men do and
strive after, and we laugh at it.

MELCHIOR. What help is that?

MORITZ. What use is help? Nothing touches us now, for good or
bad. We stand high above earthly things — each alone for
himself. We don't go with each other because it's boring. None
of us has anything it would hurt him to lose. We are infinitely
above all despair and rejoicing. We are content with ourselves,
and that is all. We despise the living so much we can hardly pity
them. They amuse us with their pretensions — and if they will
live they don't deserve to be pitied. We smile at their tragedies
— each to himself — and watch. Give me your hand! When you
give me your hand you'll fall over laughing at what happens
then —

MELCHIOR. Doesn't that disgust you?

MORITZ. We stand too high for that. We smile! At my funeral I
stood among the mourners. I quite enjoyed myself. That is
serenity, Melchior, the sublime! I howled more than anyone
and tottered to the wall holding my belly with laughing. Our
serenity is simply the attitude that allows us to swallow the

dregs. They laughed at me too, before I raised myself up to their height.

MELCHIOR. I don't want to laugh at myself.

MORITZ. The living are the last who deserve to be pitied! I admit I'd never have thought it. But now I don't know how men can be so naïve. I see through the fraud so clearly and no more doubts are left. How can you still hesitate, Melchior? Give me your hand! In less time than it takes to twist a chicken's neck you'll rise high over yourself. Your life is a sin of omission —

MELCHIOR. Can you forget?

MORITZ. We can do anything. Give me your hand! We can sorrow for youth because it takes its anxieties for ideals, and old age because stoical resolution breaks its heart. We see the emperor quake with fear at the street ballad, and the clown at the last trumpet. We see through the comedian's make-up, and watch the poet put on his mask in the dark. We look at the satisfied in all their destitution, and the capitalists toiling and groaning. We watch lovers blush before each other, when they already know they'll betray and be betrayed. We see parents bringing children into the world to be able to shout at them: how lucky you are to have such parents — and we see the children go off and do the same. We know about the innocent in their lonely passions, and we hear Schiller in the mouth of a ten-minute whore. We see God and the devil exposing themselves to ridicule in front of each other, and hold in us the unshakable conviction that they're both drunk . . . Peace, rest, Melchior! Just give me your little finger. You can be as white as snow before this moment comes again.

MELCHIOR. If I throw in my lot with you, Moritz, I do it out of self-disgust. I'm a pariah. Everything that gave me courage is in the grave. I'm incapable of any ideals — and I can see nothing, nothing that can stand in my path to the bottom. I think I'm the most disgusting creature in creation . . .

MORITZ. Why hesitate?

A MASKED MAN *comes in.*

MASKED MAN *(to* MELCHIOR). You're shivering with hunger. You're certainly in no state to decide anything. *(To* MORITZ.) Get out!

MELCHIOR. Who are you?

MASKED MAN. That will be made clear. *(To* MORITZ.) Hop it! What are you up to? Why aren't you wearing your head?

MORITZ. I shot myself.

MASKED MAN. Then stay where you belong. You're finished! Don't pester us with the stench of your grave. Incredible — look at your fingers! Filthy brute! It's already rotting.

MORITZ. Please, don't send me away —

MELCHIOR. Who are you?

MORITZ. Don't send me away. Please. Let me stay with you a little longer. I won't contradict you. It's terrible under there.

MASKED MAN. Then why all this bragging about serenity and the sublime? You know very well that's humbug — sour grapes. Why must you lie so persistently? — you — you wraith! If it means so much to you, stay as far as I'm concerned. But stop all this huffing and puffing, young man — and please don't stick your rotting thumb in my pie!

MELCHIOR. Will you tell me who you are?

MASKED MAN. No. I'll make you a proposition: put yourself in my hands. For a start, I'll do something about your present mess.

MELCHIOR. You're my father!

MASKED MAN. Wouldn't you know your dear father from his voice?

MELCHIOR. No.

MASKED MAN. Your father is at this moment seeking comfort in the strong arms of your mother. I'll open the world for you. Your temporary despair is caused by your miserable condition. With a hot dinner inside you you'll joke about it.

MELCHIOR. *(to himself)*. Only *one* of them can be the devil! *(Aloud.)* After the things I've done, a hot dinner won't give me peace again!

MASKED MAN. It depends on the dinner. One thing I will tell you, your little girl would have given birth marvellously. She was built ideally. Unfortunately, she was put down — entirely by Mother Schmidt's abortion methods. I'll take you out into the world. I'll give you the chance to widen your horizon in astonishing ways. I'll introduce you to every single interesting thing in the world.

MELCHIOR. Who are you? Who are you? I can't put myself in the hands of someone I don't know!

MASKED MAN. You only learn to know me *by* putting yourself in my hands.

MELCHIOR. Is that true?

MASKED MAN. It's a fact. And by the way, you have no choice.

MELCHIOR. I can give my hand to my friend whenever I like.

MASKED MAN. Your friend is a charlatan. No one smiles while he's still got a penny to spend in his pocket. The sublime humorist is the most miserable, pitiful creature in creation.

MELCHIOR. The humorist can be what he likes! Tell me who you are, or I'll give him my hand.

MASKED MAN. Now?

MORITZ. He's right, Melchior. I was trying it on. Take his invitation, and get everything you can out of him. It doesn't matter how well he's masked — at least he's *something!*

MELCHIOR. Do you believe in God?

MASKED MAN. Depends.

MELCHIOR. Well, tell me who invented gunpowder.

MASKED MAN. Berthold Schwarz — a Franciscan monk at Freiburg in Breisgau about 1330.

MORITZ. What wouldn't I give if he hadn't!

MASKED MAN. You'd only have hanged yourself.

MELCHIOR. What are your views on morality?

MASKED MAN. Son — am I a schoolboy?

MELCHIOR. How do I know what you are!

MORITZ. Don't quarrel. Please, don't quarrel. What's the use of that? Why sit here in the churchyard — two living and one dead — at two o'clock in the morning, if all we can do is quarrel like drunks? It will be a pleasure for me to be present at these discussions. If you want to quarrel, I'll take my head and go.

MELCHIOR. You're still the same old drag!

MASKED MAN. The ghost isn't wrong. One should never lose one's dignity. By morality I understand the real product of two imaginary forces. The imaginary forces are *should* and *would*. The product is called Morality, and no one is allowed to forget that's real.

MORITZ. If only you told me that before! My morality hounded

me to death. I used the murder weapon because of my dear
parents. "Honour thy father and mother and thy days shall be
long." The Bible certainly came unstuck over me.

MASKED MAN. You shouldn't be carried away by appearances,
my boy. Your parents would no more have died than you
needed to. Looked at clinically, they'd have raged and
stormed simply for the good of their health.

MELCHIOR. That might be true. But I can certainly tell you that
if I'd given my hand to Moritz just now, sir, that would have
been purely and simply because of my morality!

MASKED MAN. And that's exactly where you're not Moritz!

MORITZ. I don't think there's much difference — not so much
that you shouldn't have been allowed to pop up for me. I
walked slowly enough along that alder plantation with the
pistol in my pocket.

MASKED MAN. Then you don't remember me? Even in your
last moments you were still standing undecided between life
and death. But I think this is really not the best place to
prolong such a profound discussion.

MORITZ. It's certainly getting chilly. They dressed me up in my
Sunday suit but they didn't put anything on underneath.

MELCHIOR. Goodbye, Moritz. I don't know where this man will
take me. But *he* is alive . . .

MORITZ. Don't hold it against me for trying to kill you, Melchior.
It was only my old devotion. I'd spend a whole lifetime of
tears and misery, if I could walk by your side again.

MASKED MAN. In the end everyone has his part — *you* the
comforting knowledge of having nothing — *you* the tormenting
doubt of everything. Goodbye.

MELCHIOR. Goodbye, Moritz. Thank you for coming back once
more. The happy, good times we had together in those fourteen
years! I promise you whatever happens in the years to come, if
I change ten times, and go up or down, I'll never forget you . . .

MORITZ. Thank you, thank you. You were my only friend.

MELCHIOR. . . . and one day if I'm old and my hair's grey,
perhaps then you'll be closer to me again than all the people
who share my life.

MORITZ. Thank you. Good luck on the journey, gentlemen.
Don't let me keep you any longer.

MASKED MAN. Come on, young man. *(He takes* MELCHIOR's *arm and disappears with him over the graves.)*

MORITZ *(alone).* I sit here with my head in my arm. The moon covers its face, the veil falls away, and it doesn't look any wiser. So I go back to my place. I straighten my cross after that clumsy idiot's kicked it over, and when everything's in order I lie down on my back again, warm myself in my rotting decay and smile.

Methuen's Modern Plays

Methuen's Theatre Classics